VOYAGES IN ENGLISH

Writing and Grammar

Elaine de Chantal Brookes

Patricia Healey

Irene Kervick

Catherine Irene Masino

Anne B. McGuire

Adrienne Saybolt

LOYOLAPRESS.

Cover Design/Production: Loyola Press
Cover Illustration: Jeff Parks, Anni Betts
Interior Design/Production: Loyola Press, Think Design Group

Acknowledgements to copyright holders appear on page 224, which is to be
considered a continuation of the copyright page.

ISBN-10: 0-8294-2359-1
ISBN-13: 978-0-8294-2359-4

Manufactured in the United States of America.

LOYOLAPRESS.

3441 N. Ashland Avenue
Chicago, Illinois 60657
(800) 621-1008
www.loyolapress.com

Webcrafters, Inc. / Madison, WI, USA / 03-16 / 9th printing

Contents

Sentences and Personal Narratives

Stormy Night

It was a loud, rainy night.
Scary shadows were everywhere.
My chair looked like it had a
monster on it! So I turned on
the light. Then I laughed.
It was just my fuzzy bear.
It is funny to be scared
of a little, fuzzy bear.

The Sentence

A **sentence** is a group of words that expresses a complete thought.

This is not a complete sentence.

The bear

This group of words is not a sentence because it does not tell anything about the bear. A period is not placed after these words.

This is a complete sentence.

The bear ate the honey.

This group of words is a sentence because it tells what the bear did. A sentence always ends with an end mark. A period (.) is a kind of end mark.

Write an S next to each group of words that is a sentence. Put a period at the end of each sentence.

_____ 1. I made a cake

_____ 2. A kite

_____ 3. Jill gave the ball to Jenny

_____ 4. Run and hide, Bill

_____ 5. My desk

_____ 6. I rode my bike

_____ 7. The dog

_____ 8. At home

_____ 9. We made our beds

_____ 10. This is a holiday

A little black dot that you can see.
Period is my name.
A telling sentence ends with me,
I play a telling game.

Name _____

More About Sentences

A sentence begins with a **capital letter.** It ends
with an **end mark.**

● **Write these sentences correctly.**
Begin each sentence with a
capital letter. Put a period at
the end of each sentence.

1. the dog eats its dinner

   _____

   _____

2. i love to go fishing

   _____

   _____

3. amal kicks the ball

   _____

   _____

4. we walk to school

   _____

   _____

5. brandon sweeps the floor

   _____

   _____

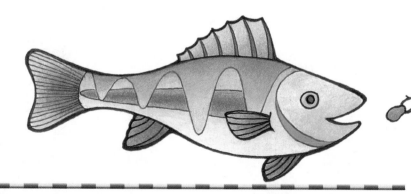

Capital Letters and End Marks

Unscramble each group of words to make a sentence. Remember to add capital letters and periods.

1. sing to she likes

2. sit sofa the on we

3. book the reads he

4. eats cookies jesse the

5. dog i give bath the a

6. runs dog the fast

7. pretty pony that is a

8. flowers they fresh bring

Name _____

Words Working Together

Words work together to build a sentence. Remember, a sentence is a group of words that expresses a complete thought.

A **Color the check mark next to each complete sentence.**

 1. Aki goes to school.

 2. gets rabbits

 3. Kylie sings with the radio.

 4. Mario watches the movie.

 5. eats an apple

 6. Andy stops the

B **Match the words in the first list with the words in the second list to build a complete sentence.**

1. The kids ● ● rises.

2. My mom ● ● plays hockey.

3. The moon ● ● fly.

4. Birds ● ● go to the park.

5. Kenji ● ● wears a green apron.

More Words Working Together

A **Match the words in the first list with the words in the second list to build a sentence. Put the correct letter on the line. The first one is done for you.**

1. The happy children   __d__   a. crashed against the rocks.

2. The baseball player   _____   b. howled through the treetops.

3. A bitter cold wind   _____   c. blazed in the fireplace.

4. Two large pine logs   _____   d. clapped their hands.

5. The big white waves   _____   e. hit a home run.

B **Match the words in the first list with the words in the second list to build a sentence.**

1. Three baby robins ●   ● chased the little mouse.

2. The big red truck ●   ● sped across the sky.

3. My playful kitten ●   ● hung in the closet.

4. Jeff's winter coat ●   ● slept in a nest.

5. A shiny silver plane ●   ● rumbled down the street.

Telling Sentences

A **telling sentence** tells about something. A period (.) is placed at the end of a telling sentence.

> *The honey is in the jar.*
> *The honey is sticky.*

Underline the complete telling sentence in each pair. Put a period at the end of each telling sentence.

1. Bob likes to fish
   Does Bob like

2. Parks his blue car
   Dad parks his car

3. Sings in the morning
   My pet bird sings

4. Beth holds the cat
   The furry cat

5. Down the busy street
   Joe runs down the street

6. The bunny is soft
   The soft little bunny

7. Leslie talks on the phone
   On the phone

8. Type on
   I type on the computer

Writer's Corner

Write a telling sentence about something you did this morning.

Name _____

Making Telling Sentences

Use the words on the right to make telling sentences.
Put a period at the end of each sentence.

1. We go to the _____

2. They feed the _____

3. Kira will not _____

4. Jason dries the _____

5. Mae rides her _____ in the park

6. Erin and Shawn play _____

7. Macon thinks _____ is fun

8. Grandma plants _____ in her garden

9. _____ scare my sister

10. Your _____ look new

11. Today it will _____

12. This _____ would make a good swing

Puppets

writing

tire

flowers

skateboard

cards

rain

park

help

shoes

birds

plates

Name _____

Commanding Sentences

A **commanding sentence** tells people what to do. A commanding sentence begins with a capital letter. A period (.) is usually placed at the end.

Stop at the red light.   *Wait for me.*

A **Color each sign that has a commanding sentence on it.**

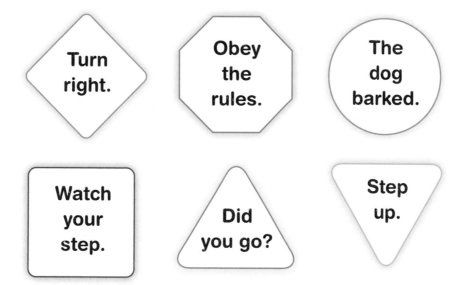

B **Put a period at the end of each commanding sentence. Underline the capital letter in the first word of each sentence.**

1. Turn off the light
2. Open the door, please
3. Work quietly
4. Swim across the pool

5. Ride your bike
6. Blow the whistle
7. Water the flowers
8. Write the answer on the line

Writer's Corner

Write a commanding sentence that you might say to someone crossing the street.

More Commanding Sentences

A Underline the commanding sentence in each pair.

1. The dog is named Bear.

   Walk the dog.

2. Help your little brother.

   Your little brother plays baseball.

3. Give Shen the cookie.

   The cookie tastes good.

4. These bags are heavy.

   Carry these bags.

B Choose the word from the word bank that best completes each commanding sentence. Remember that a sentence begins with a capital letter.

go	put	stop	don't	mow	eat

1. _____ to the kitchen.

2. _____ on your shoes.

3. _____ the lawn.

4. _____ the orange.

5. _____ banging the drum.

6. _____ pet the tiger.

Commanding Sentence is my name.
Giving directions is my aim.
I help you know the things to do
at home, at play, and in school too!

Name _____

Sentence Review

A **telling sentence** tells about something. A **commanding sentence** tells people what to do.

● **Write t beside each telling sentence. Write c beside each commanding sentence.**

1. The team is ready. __t__

2. Play ball. __c__

3. The boats are moving. _____

4. Turn off the light. _____

5. My house is on King Street. _____

6. My brother works at night. _____

7. Please sit down. _____

8. Nan likes to draw. _____

9. I read that book. _____

10. Listen to the story. _____

11. Your desk is neat. _____

12. Color the picture. _____

More Sentence Review

A Write **t** next to each telling sentence. Write **c** next to each commanding sentence.

1. Give Molly your hand. __c__

2. She can help you cross the street. __t__

3. Josh likes to read. _____

4. Take him to the library. _____

5. Let Josh pick a book. _____

6. Josh loves books about dinosaurs. _____

7. Don't let him get a scary book. _____

8. Josh also likes movies. _____

9. Josh can get one movie. _____

10. Be home by five o'clock. _____

B Write your own telling sentence.

_____

_____

_____

C Write your own commanding sentence.

_____

_____

_____

Asking Sentences

An **asking sentence** asks a question. Some asking sentences begin with **question words.** An asking sentence ends with a question mark (**?**).

Complete each sentence with a question word from the word bank. You may use some words more than once.

How	What	Who
Why	When	Where

1. _____ are you doing?

2. _____ old are you?

3. _____ did Mary laugh?

4. _____ is the picnic?

5. _____ is Pete?

I am a squiggle on your page
with a little dot below.
At the end of each asking sentence,
please place me just so.

6. _____ gave Ren that daisy?

7. _____ do we leave for the park?

8. _____ do you feed your parrot?

More Asking Sentences

A Complete each sentence with one of the question words on the right. Use each word one time.

1. _____ you going to the circus?

2. _____ Jonah popped his balloon?

3. _____ you like popcorn?

4. _____ you see the clown?

5. _____ the elephants done any tricks?

6. _____ there enough popcorn for everyone?

Do

Has

Have

Are

Is

Did

B Write the letter that tells what each sentence is.
Put the correct end mark at the end of each sentence.

t = telling   **c** = commanding   **a** = asking

_____ 1. Will you go with me

_____ 2. All fish need water

_____ 3. Today is cold

_____ 4. Does John know the way

_____ 5. Jump over the fence

Name _____

Exclaiming Sentences

An **exclaiming sentence** shows surprise or excitement. An exclamation point (!) is placed at the end of an exclaiming sentence.

What a hot day it is!   *The sun is coming out!*

○ **Underline the capital letter at the beginning of each sentence. Then put an exclamation point at the end.**

1. Watch your step

2. I am so excited

3. He can hardly wait

4. What a surprise

5. Watch out for the ball

6. The storm is coming

7. Today is my birthday

8. Look at her run

9. The bus is coming

10. This tastes delicious

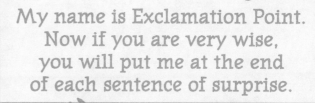

My name is Exclamation Point.
Now if you are very wise,
you will put me at the end
of each sentence of surprise.

More Exclaiming Sentences

Write your own exclaiming sentence for each picture. Remember to use an exclamation point (!).

1. _____

2. _____

3. _____

4. _____

5. _____

Writer's Corner

Write an exclaiming sentence that you might say during a thunderstorm.

Asking and Exclaiming Sentences

Read the sentences. Put a question mark at the end of each asking sentence. Put an exclamation point at the end of each exclaiming sentence.

1. How old are you

2. Can you see the clowns

3. It is so hot today

4. That is a funny mask

5. Where is my hat

6. Hurry, Paige

7. Where is the squirrel

8. Watch out

9. I had the best birthday

10. Did you read the story

More Asking and Exclaiming Sentences

Read the sentences below. Put an **X** in the Exclaiming box for each exclaiming sentence. Put an **X** in the Asking box for each asking sentence. Add the correct end mark to each sentence. The first one is done for you.

	Exclaiming	Asking
1. Where is your house **?**	☐	**X**
2. Mary did well on her test	☐	☐
3. I love my dog	☐	☐
4. How are you	☐	☐
5. It is really hot	☐	☐
6. This game is fun	☐	☐
7. Is it raining	☐	☐
8. Do you have a scooter	☐	☐
9. Who brought the kittens	☐	☐
10. When are you going home	☐	☐

Name _____

The Naming Part of a Sentence

A sentence has two parts. The **naming part** of a sentence tells who or what the sentence is about.

> _Sari likes to sing._

In this sentence the naming part is **Sari** because the sentence is about Sari.

> _The stars are very bright._

In this sentence the naming part is **The stars** because the sentence is about the stars.

Underline the naming part of each sentence.

1. We play in the snow.

2. Talia has red mittens.

3. I have a fast sled.

4. Kim makes a snow angel.

5. They make a snowman.

6. Our neighbors come over.

7. Chad makes snowballs.

8. The puppy eats snow.

9. We get cold.

10. Aunt Debbie gives us hot cocoa.

The Action Part of a Sentence

The **action part** of a sentence tells what a person or a thing does.

> *We <u>ran home</u>.*

In this sentence the action part is **ran home** because it tells what We did.

> *Jake <u>cleaned his room</u>.*

In this sentence the action part is **cleaned his room** because it tells what Jake did.

Underline the action part of each sentence.

1. The sisters watch TV.

2. Miss Burke opens the book.

3. Emil washes the dishes.

4. They play hopscotch.

5. Mr. Smith sells ice cream.

6. Kathy answers the telephone.

7. Brian plays a video game.

8. Marc runs to second base.

9. Ally helps wash the car.

10. We water the plants.

Name

Naming Parts and Action Parts

Remember that a sentence has two parts. Together, the naming part and action part form a complete sentence.

A **Match the naming part to the action part. The first one is done for you. Then say each complete sentence.**

1. She   has a pretty dress.

2. The doll   make a sandcastle.

3. The baby   sleeps in his stroller.

4. I   goes to the store.

B **Draw a line under the naming part. Draw a circle around the action part.**

1. We go to the beach.

2. My father brings a picnic.

3. I bring a pail and a shovel.

4. Grandma brings a blanket.

5. Leo makes a sandcastle.

6. Taylor and Paul go swimming.

7. My mother teaches Carly how to surf.

8. We go home after sunset.

Name _____

Show What You Know

Put the correct end mark at the end of each sentence.
Then write the letter telling what kind of sentence it is.

t = telling   c = commanding

a = asking   e = exclaiming

___t___   1. Some fish swim in the ocean .

_____   2. Will you go with me

_____   3. It is so cold

_____   4. Does Tim know how to swim

_____   5. Write your name in the book

_____   6. The green frog hopped across the pond

_____   7. Plant the seed in the ground

_____   8. That was a great game

_____   9. Do you know your teacher's name

_____   10. Don't step in that puddle

Show What You Know

Ⓐ **Read the sentences below. Underline the naming part. Circle the action part.**

1. I like peanut butter.

2. Jamal and Nico eat lunch.

3. They know where we are going.

4. Lucy and Avril pet the puppies.

5. He sees a huge spider.

Ⓑ **Write a telling sentence.**

Ⓒ **Write a commanding sentence.**

Ⓓ **Write an asking sentence.**

Ⓔ **Write an exclaiming sentence.**

What Is a Personal Narrative?

We use sentences to write stories. A personal narrative is a story about you.

A personal narrative has a **beginning**, a **middle**, and an **ending**. A personal narrative uses the words **I**, **me**, and **my**.

The Beginning

The **beginning** is the first sentence or sentences in a story. The beginning tells what the story is about.

beginning

The wind played a trick on me today. A brisk breeze took my hat and tossed it across the ground. I chased my hat and grabbed it. Would you like to have the wind treat your favorite hat this way?

Match each beginning to its story. Write the letter on the line.

a. This morning I had my first skating lesson.

b. I had fun yesterday with a cardboard box.

c. Last week I was riding my bike.

_____ Dad said it was time to take off my training wheels. I got scared. I started slowly. I pedaled once. I pedaled twice. I couldn't believe it. I was riding all by myself!

_____ As soon as I moved onto the ice, my feet slid out from under me! My coach helped me up and we started over. I wonder if penguins have this much trouble.

_____ I made it into a sled. Down a hill I zoomed on my simple sled. What an exciting ride!

The Middle

The **middle** tells what happens in the story.
A story usually has more than one middle sentence.

middle

It was my very first balloon ride. The giant, colorful balloon began to float. People waved to me from the ground. The balloon went higher and higher. Someday I'd like to go around the world in a balloon.

Read the beginning and ending sentences below. Write your own middle sentences. Use the word bank for help.

| splash | sun | turtle | fish | swim | boat |

My Day at the Lake

I had a great day at the lake.

I had so much fun that I can't wait to go back again.

The Ending

The **ending** is the last sentence or sentences in a story. The ending finishes the story. It may tell the last thing that happens, ask a question, or tell about a special feeling the writer has.

My brother and I were making cookies. He challenged me to an egg-cracking contest. He neatly cracked an egg with one hand. Then it was my turn. The whole egg, shell and all, plopped into the cookie dough. **I lost the contest, but the cookies were still delicious!**

ending

Choose the correct ending for each story. Write the letter on the line.

Nothing tastes better than lemonade on a warm day. My brother and I decided to make some. He cut up the lemons. I squeezed the lemons into a jar. Then I added sugar and water. Dad tasted it and made a funny face. _____

I learned a lot about camping last summer. Owls were hooting all night. Chirping birds woke me up in the morning. _____

Today was my first time on a subway train. We moved so fast that I could barely stand. I had to hold on tight. In the tunnel it got dark. _____

a. I cannot wait to ride again.

b. I learned that the forest is a noisy place to sleep!

c. I think I will add more sugar next time!

Write a Story

A personal narrative is a story about you. You are the star in your story. Remember to use the words **I**, **me**, and **my** to show that the story is about you.

● **Write a story about a day you remember well. Remember to include**

     a **beginning** that tells what the story is about.

     a **middle** that tells what happened in the story.

     an **ending** that tells the last thing that happened, asks a question, or tells a special feeling.

Beginning   I remember the day I _____

_____

_____

Middle _____

_____

Ending   It was the _____ day ever.

Writer's Workshop

PREWRITING

Pick a Topic

A personal narrative is a story about you. The topic can be anything that happened to you.

my trip to Florida

my first day of school

my very scary night

the time I won the contest

Raj needs to pick a topic for a personal narrative. Look at his notes.

Write a personal narrative about you. It should be a real story that happened to you. Jot down ideas in your notebook. Think about a time that

- **you were happy**

- **you were really surprised**

- **something funny happened**

- **you were scared by something silly**

Write down as many ideas as you can. Then circle the idea you like best. This will be your topic.

PREWRITING

Plan Your Story

Now Raj must plan his personal narrative. He draws pictures to help him plan his story. He draws pictures of the beginning, the middle, and the ending of his story.

Beginning

Middle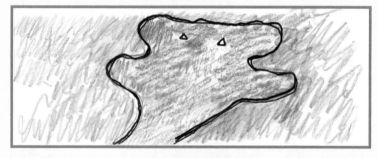

Ending

What pictures come to mind when you think of your story? Draw in your notebook pictures of the beginning, the middle, and the ending. Write **Beginning** next to the beginning pictures. Write **Middle** next to the middle pictures. Write **Ending** next to the ending pictures.

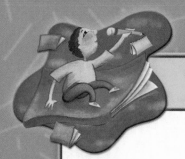

Writer's Workshop

DRAFTING

When you first write your narrative, you are drafting.
This is Raj's draft.

> My chair looked like it had a monster on it! So I on the light. Then I laughed. It was just my fuzzy bear. It is funny to be scared of a little, fuzzy bear.

Look at the pictures you drew. Make sure that they are in the right order. Draw more pictures if you need to. Then write a sentence to go with each picture.

Write your draft in your notebook. Use your pictures and sentences to help you. You can also use the words in the word bank if you need help. Remember to write a beginning, a middle, and an ending.

surprise	happy	loud	shiny
scary	warm	fuzzy	laugh

EDITING

When you check your draft, you are editing. Raj uses this Editing Checklist to check his draft.

I don't have a beginning.

Editing Checklist

- ☐ Do I have a beginning?
- ☐ Do I have a middle?
- ☐ Do I have an ending?
- ☐ Is my story about me?
- ☐ Is my story in order?

It was a loud, rainy night. Scary shadows were everywhere. ∧My chair looked like it had a monster on it! So I on the light.

Look at the mistake Raj finds. How does he fix it?

Look at your draft. Then use the checklist. If you spot a mistake, fix it. You might ask a friend to read your story. Friends can help spot mistakes.

REVISING

Raj copies his draft. He adds changes that make the draft better.

Copy your story. Add any changes that will make it better. Fix any mistakes that you find. Make your story the best it can be.

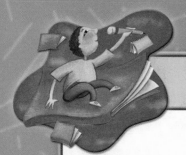

Writer's Workshop

PROOFREADING

When you check your words and sentences, you are proofreading.
Raj uses this Proofreading Checklist to check his draft.

Proofreading Checklist

☐ Are all the words spelled correctly?

☐ Did I use capital letters?

☐ Did I use the right end marks?

☐ Are the sentences complete?

It was a loud, rainy night.

Scary shadows were everywhere.

My chair looked like it had a
*   turned*
monster on it! So I∧on the light.

Look at the mistake that Raj finds. How does he fix it?

Use the checklist to check your draft. Put an **X** next to the questions
you can answer yes to. Use these proofreading marks to mark
your changes.

Proofreading Marks		
Symbol	**Meaning**	**Example**
∧	add	We∧books. read
⟲	take out	the the park
⊙	add period	She is smart⊙
≡	capital letter	carl jones
/	lowercase letter	He likes Soccer.

PUBLISHING

When you share your work, you are publishing it. It is an exciting time. Your readers are seeing your very best work.

How will Raj publish his draft?

Are you ready to share your work? Copy your story onto a sheet of paper. Print as neatly as you can. Be sure to copy it exactly. Leave room to draw a picture.

You can share your story in many ways. How will you share yours?

I want to read my story to my mom!

Make a book.

Give it to my parents.

Put it on the bulletin board.

Stormy Night
It was a loud, rainy night.
Scary shadows were everywhere.
My chair looked like it had a
monster on it! So I turned on
the light. Then I laughed.
It was just my fuzzy bear.
It's funny to be scared.
Hello, fuzzy bear.

Make it into a skit.

Read it to a friend.

Frame it.

Decide with your class how to share your story. Come up with new and fun ways.

Remember to keep thinking of new story ideas!

Nouns and Friendly Letters

Quotation Station

Words have no wings,
but they can fly
thousands of miles.

—Korean proverb

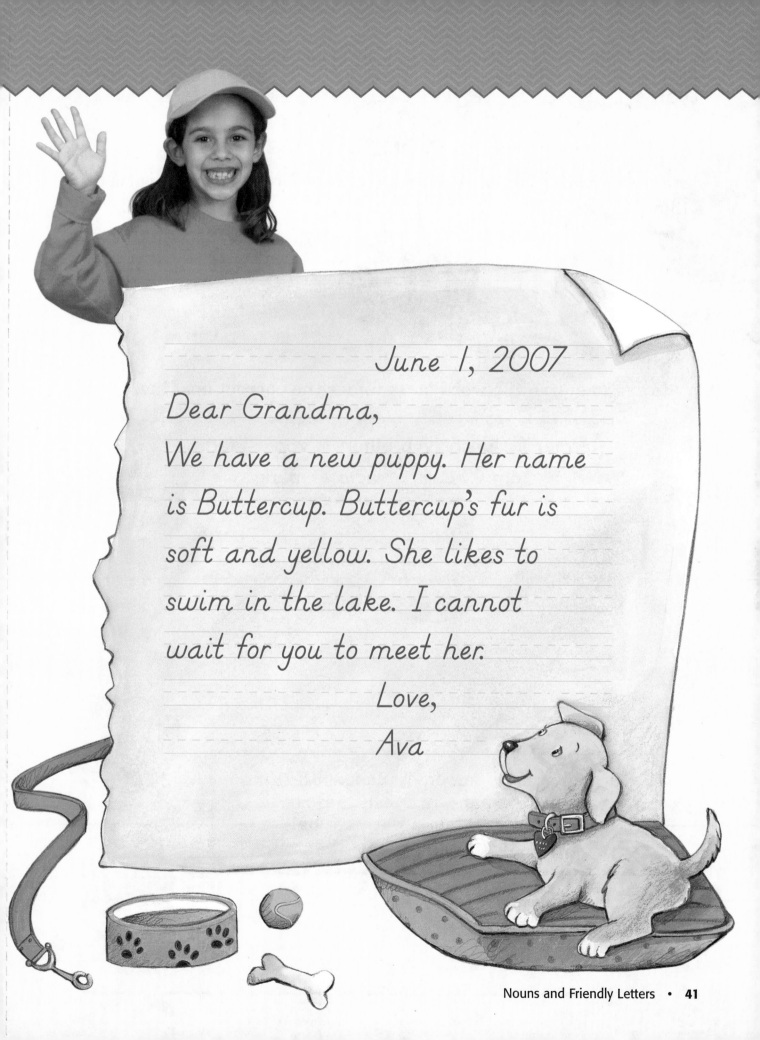

June 1, 2007

Dear Grandma,

We have a new puppy. Her name is Buttercup. Buttercup's fur is soft and yellow. She likes to swim in the lake. I cannot wait for you to meet her.

Love,

Ava

Nouns

A **noun** can name a person. A noun can name a place. A noun can name a thing.

Write each noun in the word bank under the correct heading.

| farmer | lunch | brother | zoo | farm |
| Tom | ball | radio | park | |

Person	**Place**	**Thing**

A noun names a person, a place, or a thing—
a friend, the park, or a bell that rings,
a boy, a building, a bat, or a ball.
Nouns are words that name them all.

More Nouns

Does the underlined noun name a person, a place, or a thing?
Circle the answer.

1. Earth is a <u>planet</u>. **person   place   (thing)**

2. The <u>rooster</u> crowed at dawn. **person   place   thing**

3. The boats sail on the <u>lake</u>. **person   place   thing**

4. The <u>robot</u> belongs to me. **person   place   thing**

5. We pick flowers in the <u>garden</u>. **person   place   thing**

6. <u>Tito</u> saw a skunk. **person   place   thing**

7. A <u>comet</u> has appeared. **person   place   thing**

8. My <u>dad</u> plays basketball. **person   place   thing**

9. I took a walk in the <u>park</u>. **person   place   thing**

10. My <u>sister</u> likes to read. **person   place   thing**

Writer's Corner

Write a sentence about a person you know. Use a noun.

Name _____

Proper Nouns

A **proper noun** can name a special person. A proper noun can name a special place. A proper noun can name a special thing. A proper noun always begins with a capital letter.

*Who is that **girl**?*   *Oh, that is **Maya**.*

A **Write each proper noun from the word bank under the correct heading.**

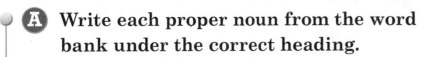

Mayflower	United States	Liberty Bell
Florida	Julie	Steve

Person	**Place**	**Thing**

B **Find the name of the special person, place, or thing in each sentence. Underline the proper noun. Circle the capital letter that begins each proper noun.**

1. Miami is a big city.

2. Tara had a birthday party.

3. Did you see the Statue of Liberty?

4. When did you visit Italy?

5. Jory is my brother.

6. Do they like Texas?

The Days of the Week

The names of the days of the week are proper nouns. The name of each day begins with a capital letter.

Sunday	Monday	Tuesday	Wednesday	Thursday	Friday	Saturday

Write the day that answers the question.

1. What is the last day of the week?

2. On what day does the week begin?

3. What is the third day of the week?

4. On what day do you start school?

5. What day comes after Thursday?

6. What is the fourth day of the week?

7. What day comes before Friday?

Name _____

Practice the Days of the Week

Look at the weather forecast. Answer the questions about the weather. Remember, the names of the days of the week are proper nouns. A proper noun begins with a capital letter.

Sunday	Monday	Tuesday	Wednesday	Thursday	Friday	Saturday
20°	27°	33°	30°	33°	40°	50°

1. On which day will it snow? _____

2. Which will be the warmest day of the week? _____

3. Which day will be very cloudy? _____

4. Which is the last day it will be 33°? _____

5. Which day will be a little cloudy? _____

6. Which day will reach 40°? _____

7. Which day of the week will be the coldest? _____

The Months of the Year

The months of the year have special names. They are proper nouns. The name of each month begins with a capital letter.

Trace the names of the months of the year. Begin with January and work down.

January   July

February   August

March   September

April   October

May   November

June   December

30 days has September,
April, June, and November.
All the rest have 31
except for February, which has 28,
and 29 in a leap year,
which is great!

Writer's Corner

Write a sentence that tells when your birthday is.

Name _____

Practice the Months of the Year

Complete each sentence with the name of a month of the year.
Remember that each month begins with a capital letter.

January	April	July	October
February	May	August	November
March	June	September	December

1. In **N** ____ **vem** ____ ____ ____ we celebrate Thanksgiving.

2. ____ **anu** ____ ____ ____ brings a new year.

3. Halloween is in ____ **c** ____ **o** ____ ____ ____ .

4. On the Fourth of ____ ____ ____ **y**, we see a lot of fireworks.

5. We give Valentine's Day cards in **F** ____ ____ **ru** ____ ____ **y**.

6. Labor Day is in **S** ____ ____ **tem** ____ ____ ____ .

7. In ____ **p** ____ ____ ____ there is a lot of rain.

8. The Easter Bunny will visit in ____ ____ **rc** ____ .

9. **D** ____ **cem** ____ ____ ____ is the last month.

10. Father's Day is in ____ ____ **n** ____ .
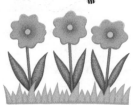

11. Flowers bloom during ____ ____ ____ .

12. ____ **ugu** ____ ____ is usually the hottest month of the year.

Abbreviations

An **abbreviation** is a short form of a word. An abbreviation usually begins with a capital letter. Most abbreviations are followed by a period.

A **Each day of the week has an abbreviation. Match each day to its abbreviation.**

Sunday   Monday   Tuesday   Wednesday   Thursday   Friday   Saturday

Wed.   Sat.   Mon.   Sun.   Tues.   Fri.   Thurs.

B **Some months of the year have abbreviations. Trace each one.**

January *Jan.*   February *Feb.*   March *Mar.*

April *Apr.*   August *Aug.*   September *Sept.*

October *Oct.*   November *Nov.*   December *Dec.*

C **Abbreviations are used for titles of people. Trace each title.**

Dr. Brooks   *Mrs.* Adams   *Mr.* Conroy

D **Write the abbreviation for each of these words.**

October _____   Doctor _____   Monday _____

March _____   Mister _____   Thursday _____

Initials

An **initial** takes the place of a person's name. An initial is the first letter in a name. An initial is always a capital letter. An initial is followed by a period.

Miles Lee Carr **M.L.C.**   *Ella Ann Howe* **E.A.H.**

A **Underline the abbreviation or the initials in each sentence. Place a period after each abbreviation or after each initial.**

1. Mr Ward works in that skyscraper.

2. Jan is the abbreviation for January.

3. C M S are my initials.

4. Dr Adams will arrive soon.

5. Tues is the abbreviation for Tuesday.

B **Write the initial for each name. Use a capital letter and a period.**

Susan _____   Mark Garcia _____

Christopher _____   Becca Wilson _____

C **Write your initials after your name at the top of this page.**

Name _____

Common Nouns

A **common noun** can name any person. A common noun can name any
place. A common noun can name any thing.

A **Read the noun in each present. Color the present blue if the
noun names a person. Make the present pink if the noun names
a place. Color the present yellow if the noun names a thing.**

B **Complete each sentence with a noun from the presents.**

1. We have many _____ .

2. Who is that _____ ?

3. We read books in the _____ .

4. I drink _____ every day.

5. Please close the _____ .

6. My _____ makes dinner for our family.

7. Kim and Matt went to play in the _____ .

8. The _____ has many cars and buses.

Common Nouns and Proper Nouns

A **common noun** names any person, place, or thing.
A **proper noun** names a special person, place, or thing.

girl   *Maggie*

Girl is a common noun. **Maggie** is a proper noun.

Complete each sentence with a noun from the word bank. If the word is a proper noun, write **p**. If the word is a common noun, write **c**.

Wood School	**ladder**	**igloo**	**wind**
Morris Library	**smoke**	**Janice**	**breakfast**

1. *Smoke*   is coming from the chimney.   **c**

2. _____ has story hour today. _____

3. A strong _____ blew the hat away. _____

4. _____ rode a bus. _____

5. We eat _____ every morning. _____

6. _____ is closed today. _____

7. Kevin's _____ melted. _____

8. Firefighters climbed up the _____ . _____

Singular and Plural Nouns

When a noun names one, it is **singular**. When a noun names more than one, it is **plural**. Add the letter **s** to make most nouns plural.

A Look at the picture. Circle the nouns that are plural.

B Underline the correct noun and write it on the line.

1. Linda has two new _____ . (hat hats)

2. Mom made a _____ for lunch. (salads salad)

3. All the _____ are white. (duck ducks)

4. Sandy drew a pretty _____ . (picture pictures)

5. That is my favorite _____ . (song songs)

More Singular and Plural Nouns

Read the sentences below. Then look at the underlined nouns. If the noun is singular, put an **X** in the first box. If the noun is plural, put an **X** in the second box.

	Singular	Plural
1. I have a basket of <u>apples</u>.	☐	☐
2. My sister has a cool <u>bike</u>.	☐	☐
3. I hear a loud <u>bell</u>.	☐	☐
4. Are the <u>baseballs</u> in the closet?	☐	☐
5. Sarah has three <u>dogs</u>.	☐	☐
6. I see two <u>cars</u>.	☐	☐
7. Mr. Wade wrote a <u>book</u>.	☐	☐
8. We made a <u>cake</u> for the bake sale.	☐	☐
9. Where are the <u>girls</u>?	☐	☐
10. Did you bring my <u>CD</u>?	☐	☐

Writer's Corner

Write about some animals you like. Use a plural noun.

Name _____

Possessives

A **possessive noun** shows ownership. Here is a way to show possession.

Claire has homework.   *It is **Claire's** homework.*
Aaron has a dog.   *It is **Aaron's** dog.*
The kitten has a tail.   *It is the **kitten's** tail.*

Add an apostrophe and s (**'s**) to show ownership.

A **Underline the word in each sentence that shows possession.**

1. The lion's paw had a thorn in it.

2. Is Ben's picture in the newspaper?

3. Marcy's gerbil won first prize.

4. Kim's crayons were brand new.

5. The bear's fur is dark brown.

B **Write the correct possessive noun.**

1. Anita has books. They are  *Anita's* books.

2. The bull has horns. They are the _____ horns.

3. The nurse has a cap. It is the _____ cap.

4. The bird has wings. They are the _____ wings.

5. The boy has an eraser. It is the _____ eraser.

Singular Possessives

A singular noun names one person or animal.

    girl   *Tony*   *tiger*

An apostrophe and s (**'s**) are used to show possession when the noun is singular.

    girl's   *Tony's*   *tiger's*

Write the singular possessive of each word on the line. Remember to use an apostrophe and s ('s).

spider	principal	Ryan	Linda
teacher	child	owl	

1. _____ ponytail blew in the wind.

2. Are _____ gloves on the shelf?

3. Did anyone see the _____ glue stick?

4. An _____ eyes are very large.

5. A _____ web is often sticky.

6. The _____ toy was under the table.

7. The _____ message was loud and clear.

Plural Possessives

A plural noun names more than one person or animal.

boys   *lions*

To show that more than one person or animal owns something, add only an apostrophe (') to most plural nouns.

the girls have dolls   *the **girls'** dolls*

our dogs have food   *our **dogs'** food*

the teachers have a room   *the **teachers'** room*

In each sentence underline the noun that shows that more than one person or animal owns something.

1. The rabbits' tails are short and stumpy.

2. My sisters' rooms are never in order.

3. The boys' voices echoed in the cave.

4. Can you find the foxes' tracks?

5. The students' papers hung on the bulletin board.

To show belonging and ownership,
a possessive is what to use.
An apostrophe and the letter s
will tell you whose is whose.

Writer's Corner

Write two sentences with plural possessives.

Name _____

Possessive Practice

● **Write the possessive for each sentence.**

1. The monkeys have a cage. It is the *monkeys'* cage.

2. The birds have a nest. It is the _____ nest.

3. My brothers have cars. They are my _____ cars.

4. The girls have sweaters. They are the _____ sweaters.

5. The cats have ears. They are the _____ ears.

6. The students have desks. They are the _____ desks.

7. The teams have bats. They are the _____ bats.

8. The bears have a cave. It is the _____ cave.

9. The boys wear hats. They are the _____ hats.

10. My friends have books. They are my _____ books.

Name _____

Compound Words

A **compound word** is a word that is made by putting two words together.

bluebird   *raincoat*   *hairbrush*

The word **bluebird** is made by putting together the words **blue** and **bird**. What words are put together to make **raincoat** and **hairbrush**?

Underline the compound word in each sentence. Write the two words that make up the compound word. The first one is done for you.

1. We made <u>cupcakes</u>.   *cup*   *cakes*

2. Chris bought a birdhouse.

3. My aunt is a firefighter.

4. Look at that huge waterfall.

5. My birthday is tomorrow!

6. This is a big airport.

7. Did you see that earthworm?

More Compound Words

Make a compound word by choosing the right word from each list. Then write the compound word on the line. The first one is done for you.

1. book *store* *bookstore*
   look
   store
   brush

2. door
   hand
   hammer
   mat

3. camp
   tree
   fire
   burger

4. mail
   box
   card
   paper

5. shoe
   stone
   shirt
   lace

When you join two words together, you make a compound word. *Butterfly, snowball,* and *bluebird* are compound words that you have heard.

Name _____

Practice Compound Words

A Answer each riddle with a compound word. Use the words in the word bank to make compound words.

guard	paper	hook	print

1. I am at the end of a fishing line.

   What am I?   a fish _____

2. I bring news to people every day.

   What am I?   a news _____

3. I leave my mark on wet sand.

   What am I?   a foot _____

4. I work at beaches and swimming pools.

   I save people's lives. Who am I?   a life _____

B Match each word in the first list with a word in the second list to make compound words.

1. bird _____   **ball**

2. air _____   **house**

3. thunder _____   **cloth**

4. basket _____   **storm**

5. table _____   **plane**

Name _____

Show What You Know

A Look at the underlined noun in each sentence. Write **p** on the line if the noun is a proper noun. Write **c** on the line if the noun is a common noun.

1. A <u>camel</u> does not need much water. _____

2. It can travel through the <u>desert</u>. _____

3. <u>Adam</u> can ride a camel. _____

4. He rides it through the <u>Sahara</u>. _____

5. His camel has two <u>humps</u>. _____

B Write the day of the week or the month of the year.

1. What day of the week begins with **M**? _____

2. What day of the week begins with **F**? _____

3. Christmas comes during which month? _____

4. Which is a summer month? _____

5. What month of the year begins with **M**? _____

C Write the abbreviation for each word.

1. Doctor _____   3. September _____

2. Tuesday _____   4. Monday _____

Name _____

Show What You Know

A **Write the initial for each underlined name.**

1. <u>Rose</u> Waters _____   3. <u>Brian</u> Taylor _____

2. John <u>Paul</u> Jones _____   4. Zoe <u>Mary</u> Ward _____

B **Underline the plural noun in each group.**

1. cat, dog, kittens, lion   3. paper, eraser, pencils, crayon

2. girls, boy, child, girl   4. tail, kite, string, trees

C **Write a shorter way of showing possession for the underlined words.**

1. The <u>finger Maria has</u> was cut.   _____ finger

2. The <u>shoe Brad has</u> fell off.   _____ shoe

3. The <u>eyes the piglets have</u> are shut.   _____ eyes

4. The <u>rolls the baker has</u> are fresh.   _____ rolls

D **Choose a word that best completes each compound word.**

where	berry	cut	dream

1. blue_____   3. some_____

2. day_____   4. hair_____

Get Ready to Write

What Is a Friendly Letter?

Everyone loves to get a letter. Friendly letters are letters to people we know. Here are some things you can write in a friendly letter.

○ **Share a story or a message.**

> I scored a goal today!

Say thank you.

> Thanks for taking me to the park.

Ask a favor.

> Can you teach me how to skate?

○ **Imagine that you are going to write a letter. What are some things you might say? Write an example for each.**

Share a story or a message.

_____

_____

Say thank you.

_____

_____

Ask a favor.

_____

_____

The Parts of a Friendly Letter

Friendly letters have five parts.

Date ———————————————————— March 28, 2007

Greeting ———————— Dear Ms. Lee,

Body ——————————— Thank you for making cupcakes for our class party. They were delicious. We had so much fun playing games and having snacks. Thank you for thinking of us.

Closing ——————————————— Your friend,

Signature ——————————————— Mr. Cooper

Look at the letter. Then answer the questions.

1. What is the date of the letter?

2. Who wrote the letter?

3. What is the greeting?

4. Which part of the letter says thank you?

5. What is the closing?

The Five Parts

A friendly letter has five parts.

The **date** tells when the letter was written. The **greeting** tells who the letter is for. The **body** is the message of the letter. The **closing** says goodbye. The **signature** is the name of the person who wrote the letter.

(A) **Match each part in the first list to its part in the second list.**

1. date   ●   ● Dear Luke,

2. greeting   ●   ● Gavin

3. body   ●   ● Your friend,

4. closing   ●   ● August 9, 2007

5. signature   ●   ● Can you come to my sleepover?

(B) **Name each part of a letter by writing the correct number in the box.**

1. body   **2. signature**   **3. greeting**

4. closing   **5. date**

☐ January 21, 2007

☐ Dear Gina,

☐ I am sorry you are not feeling well. Will you be back soon? We are doing some fun projects in school. We all miss you.

☐ Your friend,

☐ Rebecca

Putting the Letter Together

These parts of a letter are mixed up. Write the letter correctly. Then write in the boxes the names of the parts of a letter. One is done for you.

| body | signature | greeting | closing | date |

Brandon

Your cousin,

That book you read sounds cool! May I borrow it? I promise to return it as soon as I am done.

Dear Kira,

August 10, 2008

Signature Brandon

Writer's Workshop

PREWRITING

Pick a Topic

Friendly letters are letters to people we know. The letter can share a story or a message. It can say thank you. It can ask a favor.

Ava must think of to whom she will write. She also must think about the topic of her letter. Look at Ava's notes.

Friendly letters say different things. They can

share a story or a message.

say thank you.

ask a favor.

tell Grandma about our new puppy

thank Mr. Bernal for the book

ask Jayden to lend me her new video game

Write down as many ideas as you can.
Write who your letter will be to.
Then circle the idea you like best.
This will be your topic.

PREWRITING

Plan Your Letter

Now Ava must plan her letter. She makes a chart to help. She makes sure that her chart has the five parts of a friendly letter.

Date: June 7, 2007
Greeting: Dear Grandma,

Body: got puppy
      soft
      yellow
      likes to swim

Closing: Love,
Signature: Ava

Make a plan in your notebook. Draw a chart like the one Ava made. Be sure to include a **date**, a **greeting**, a **body**, a **closing**, and a **signature**. Write your plan in the chart.

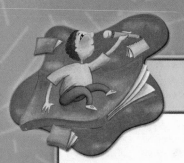

Writer's Workshop

DRAFTING

This is Ava's draft.

> Dear Grandma,
>
> We have a new puppy. Her name is Buttercup. Buttercups fur is soft and yellow. She likes to swim in the lake. I cannot wait for you to meet her.
>
> Love,
>
> Ava

Look at your chart. Make sure that you have all the parts of a friendly letter. If you think of other things to say, add them to your plan.

Write your draft in your notebook. Use your chart to help you. Remember to include all five parts of a friendly letter.

EDITING

Ava uses this Editing Checklist to check her draft.

Dear Grandma, ∧*June 1, 2007*

We have a new puppy. Her name is

Look at the mistake Ava finds. How does she fix it?

Use the checklist to edit your letter. Check for one thing at a time. Think about ways to make your letter great. Remember, you can always make more changes later.

I forgot to put the date in!

REVISING

Ava copies her letter. She adds changes that make it better.

Copy your letter. Make it better than it was before. Add anything from the checklist that you forgot. Add anything that will make your letter a great letter.

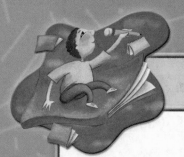

Writer's Workshop

PROOFREADING

Ava knows she can make her letter even better. She can make sure that her words and sentences are right. She uses this Proofreading Checklist to check her draft.

Look at the mistake that Ava finds. How does she fix it?

Proofreading Checklist

☐ Are all the words spelled correctly?

☐ Did I use capital letters?

☐ Did I use the right end marks?

☐ Did I use nouns correctly?

June 1, 2007

Dear Grandma,

We have a new puppy. Her name is

Buttercup. Buttercup's fur is soft and

Read your story again. Is it better than it was before? Can you answer yes to the questions on the checklist? Put an **X** next to the questions you can answer yes to. If you cannot answer yes, change your draft until you can put an **X** next to the question.

PUBLISHING

When you share your work, you are publishing it. It is an exciting time. Your readers are seeing your very best work.

How will Ava publish her draft?

Copy your letter onto a sheet of paper. Write neatly. Copy everything exactly. Be sure you have all five parts of a letter.

You might draw a picture to go with your letter. Did you thank someone for a new toy? Draw a picture of the toy. Did you write a letter about your new home? Draw a picture of your new home.

The best part about writing a letter is sharing it. How will you share your letter?

I'm going to mail my letter to Grandma!

Deliver it to the person you wrote it to.

Send it to a friend in your class.

Put it on the bulletin board.

Give it to your parents.

Make a classroom mailbox.

Decide with your class how to share your letter. Come up with new and fun ways. And keep writing letters to people you know!

Verbs and How-to Articles

How to Make an Ice-Cream Sundae

Ice-cream sundaes are fun to make and to eat.

What You Need

bowl   whipped cream

ice cream   cherry   chocolate sauce

Steps

1. First put a scoop of ice cream in a bowl.

2. Next cover the ice cream with chocolate sauce.

3. Then put on some whipped cream.

4. Last top with a big cherry.

Is your mouth watering yet? Go ahead and eat!

Action Verbs

A **verb** is a word that shows action. You cannot have a sentence without a verb.

You do many actions during the day. You walk, talk, play, and read. *Walk, talk, play,* and *read* are action verbs.

Underline the verb in each sentence. Then write the verb on the line.

1. The bell <u>rings</u>. *rings*

2. The duck waddles. _____

3. Birds fly. _____

4. Rabbits hop. _____

5. Dogs bark. _____

6. The horse gallops. _____

7. Our canary sings. _____

8. Babies laugh. _____

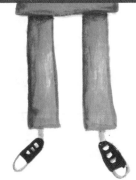

Run and *jump* and *play* and *sing*—
these are action words.
When you want to show what
happens, use an action verb.

Writer's Corner

Write a sentence about an action you like to do. Use one of the verbs above if you need help.

More Action Verbs

Many verbs are action words. In speaking and writing, you use many different action words.

A **Complete each sentence with a verb on the right.**

1. At the ball game, we _____ hot dogs.

2. Did he _____ with you?

3. The farmer _____ the horses some hay.

4. Our dog _____ his nose.

5. Jack _____ here to see us.

6. Yesterday our club _____ to the museum.

7. Our teacher _____ us to see the aquarium.

8. The fan _____ the papers across the room.

scratched
gave
went
ate
blew
came
took
come

B **Write two sentences. Use a verb from the fish in each sentence.**

1. _____

2. _____

Verbs in the Present Tense

Some verbs tell what happens often. When a verb tells what **one** person or thing does often, add the letter **s**. When a verb tells what **two or more** people or things do often, do not add the letter **s**.

one:

*Devin **reads** every day.*

more than one:

*Rene and Ana **read** after dinner.*

Ⓐ Complete each sentence with the correct verb on the right.

1. Dave _____ to the teacher.

2. The men _____ houses.

3. Gerry _____ rope.

4. The door _____ wide.

open	opens
jump	jumps
paint	paints
listen	listens

Ⓑ Find in each sentence the verb in the present tense. Write the verb on the line. If it ends in **s**, circle the **s**.

1. Casper barks every night.   *bark(s)*

2. Beth and I hear him in our bedroom. _____

3. Casper covers his eyes with his paws. _____

4. He sees the moon in the sky. _____

Name _____

Has and Have

Has and **have** are verbs in the present tense.

Has is used when you speak about **one** person, place, or thing.

> *Tommy **has** a guitar.*

Have is used when you speak about **more than one** person, place, or thing.

> *Sato and Mari **have** a new kitten.*

Have is also used with the words **I** and **you**.

> *I **have** a toothache.*   *You **have** a funny mask.*

A **Underline the correct verb to complete each sentence. The first one is done for you.**

1. Chuck (<u>has</u> have) a kite.
2. Plants (has have) roots.
3. The castle (has have) a tower.
4. A dog (has have) four legs.
5. You (has have) blue eyes.
6. An orange (has have) vitamin C.

B **Write has or have to complete each sentence.**

1. Do you _____ any pets?
2. I _____ a funny poem.
3. The salad _____ tomatoes in it.
4. This cow _____ a calf.
5. I _____ a purple skateboard.

Verbs in the Past Tense

Some verbs tell what happened in the past. Add the letters **ed** to most verbs to make them tell action in the past.

present:

*The girls **walk** the dog every morning.*

past:

*The girls **walked** the dog yesterday.*

If a verb ends in a silent **e**, drop the **e** before adding the letters **ed**.

*dance   danc**ed***

Complete each sentence with a verb from the word bank.

> **leaked   wiggled   filled**
>
> **climbed   laughed**

1. Water _____ out of the pipe.

2. Alex _____ the water jug.

3. The boys _____ at the clowns.

4. A worm _____ on the beach.

5. The tiger _____ the tree.

More Verbs in the Past Tense

Some verbs tell what happened in the past. If a verb ends with a consonant following a vowel, the consonant is usually doubled before adding the letters **ed**.

skip   skip**ped**

A Drop the silent **e** and add the letters **ed** to each verb. Write the verb on the line.

1. smile _____   3. like _____

2. tape _____   4. hope _____

B Double the final consonant and add the letters **ed** to each verb. Write the verb on the line.

1. mop _____   4. step _____

2. hop _____   5. beg _____

3. jog _____   6. trim _____

Writer's Corner

Write a sentence about something you did yesterday.
Use a verb in the past tense.

Working with Verbs

A The first sentence tells about something that happens often. Complete the second sentence with a verb that tells what happened in the past. Use the word bank.

| beeped | burned | crossed | licked | sailed |

1. The boat <u>sails</u> on the water.   The boat _____ on the water.

2. The children <u>cross</u> the street.   The children _____ the street.

3. The cat <u>licks</u> her paws.   The cat _____ her paws.

4. The driver <u>beeps</u> his horn.   The driver _____ his horn.

5. The candle <u>burns</u> slowly.   The candle _____ slowly.

B Write **has** or **have** to complete each sentence.

1. Josh _____ a new backpack.

2. You _____ never seen a whale?

3. I _____ a pet turtle.

4. The American flag _____ 50 stars.

More Work with Verbs

A **Add the letters** ed **to make the verb past tense.**

1. Yesterday I _____ on the phone. **talk**

2. Sarah _____ berries. **pick**

3. I _____ the dog yesterday. **walk**

4. Last week I _____ a tree. **climb**

B **Drop the silent** e **and add the letters** ed.

1. The baby _____ at me. **smile**

2. My uncle _____ in France. **live**

3. Sue _____ oatmeal cookies. **bake**

4. Allison _____ her brother. **tickle**

C **Double the final consonant and add the letters** ed.

1. Scott _____ to see you after school. **stop**

2. Everyone _____ after the band played. **clap**

3. Min _____ a penny into the well. **drop**

4. I _____ the banana in chocolate. **dip**

Hurrah for Helping Verbs

A **helping verb** helps another verb tell the action in the sentence.

*Jamie **will catch** some big fish.*

The verb is **catch**. The helping verb is **will**.

A **Circle the helping verb in each sentence. The verb it helps is underlined.**

1. A beaver can <u>make</u> the most interesting hideout.

2. Its home is <u>made</u> of sticks and stones.

3. You will <u>find</u> the beaver's home in a stream.

4. A beaver will <u>repair</u> its home at night.

5. This beaver was <u>building</u> a home.

B **Complete each sentence with a helping verb from the word bank.**

may	am	are	will	have

1. The fish _____ swimming.

2. I _____ running in the track race.

3. It _____ rain on our picnic tomorrow.

4. Pogo _____ hide in his doghouse during storms.

5. The cows _____ stood for an hour under the tree.

Is and was and will and can—these verbs help other verbs. When the action in a sentence needs a hand, you use a helping verb.

Verbs That Tell What Is Happening Now

Some verbs show an action that is happening now. Add the letters **ing** to show an action that is happening now. Use the helping verbs **am, is,** or **are.**

jump   *jump**ing***

*The dolphins **are jumping** in the water.*

Show that these actions are happening now. Add the letters ing to each verb.

1. Who is _____ the door? **answer**

2. We are _____ the boat. **sail**

3. I am _____ to the radio. **listen**

4. May I ask who is _____ ? **call**

5. The girls are _____ pictures. **paint**

6. Who are you _____ to? **point**

7. Hallie and Ashley are _____ . **talk**

8. Heather is _____ the piano. **play**

Writer's Corner

Write a sentence about something you see now. Use a verb with the letters *ing.*

More Things That Are Happening Now

When a verb ends in a silent **e**, drop the **e** before adding the letters **ing**. Remember to use the helping verbs **is, am,** and **are**.

We dance.   *We are danc**ing.***

When a verb ends with a consonant following a vowel, the consonant is usually doubled before adding the letters **ing**.

She skips.   *She is skipp**ing.***

A **Drop the silent e and add the letters ing to each verb.**

1. My aunt is _____ cookies. **bake**

2. Alex and Eli are _____ a sandcastle. **make**

3. I am _____ away. **move**

4. Brad is _____ to borrow that book. **hope**

B **Double the final consonant and add the letters ing to each verb.**

1. The dogs are _____ for a bone. **beg**

2. My brother is _____ in the rain. **jog**

3. Corn is _____ in the kitchen. **pop**

4. I am _____ pancakes. **flip**

Verbs Review

Remember that adding the letters **ing** shows that an action is happening now. If a verb ends in a silent **e**, drop the **e** and add the letters **ing**.

A **Add the letters ing to each verb.**

1. I am _____ the Nature Club.   **join**

2. An acorn is _____ from the tree.   **fall**

3. The teacher is _____ to the class.   **talk**

4. Dan is _____ the cow.   **milk**

5. What is Daryl _____ to?   **point**

B **Drop the silent e and add the letters ing to each verb.**

1. The children are _____ the leaves.   **rake**

2. Celia is _____ we will visit Gram.   **hope**

3. Uncle Al is _____ the show for us.   **tape**

4. My friends are _____ in the park.   **skate**

5. I think that dog is _____!   **smile**

More Verbs Review

If a verb ends with a consonant following a vowel, double the consonant before adding the letters **ing**.

A **Double the consonant and add the letters ing to each verb.**

1. The fish are _____ in their bowl.   **flip**

2. My dad was _____ with his friends.   **chat**

3. James and Lee are _____ the floor.   **mop**

4. The frogs are _____ really high!   **hop**

5. Why are we _____?   **stop**

B **Write a sentence about each picture. Use the verb under each picture. The verb should end in ing.**

comb

_____

_____

_____

clap

_____

_____

_____

Saw and Seen

Some verbs are not strong. They need help doing their job.

Saw is a strong verb. **Saw** never needs a helper. **Seen** is not a strong verb. **Seen** always needs a helper. Some helpers are **has, have, am, is, are, was,** and **were**.

*Alexis **has seen** the stars every night.*

A **Underline the correct verb in each sentence. Watch for helpers.**

1. Who has (saw seen) the planet Venus?

2. I (saw seen) it through a telescope.

3. The red glow around Venus was (saw seen) by Emily.

4. Jacob and Madison (saw seen) the planet Mercury.

5. Mike and Hannah have (saw seen) the rings around Saturn.

B **Write saw or seen to complete each sentence. Remember to look for helpers.**

1. Nick has _____ a shooting star.

2. Kendra _____ the comet.

3. She has _____ comets before.

4. I never _____ one.

5. Jake _____ one too.

Ate and Eaten, Gave and Given

Remember that some verbs need help doing their job. Some helpers are **has, have, am, is, are, was,** and **were**.

Ate is a strong verb. **Eaten** is not a strong verb. **Eaten** always needs a helper.

*The cat **has eaten** the cheese.*

Gave is a strong verb. **Given** is not a strong verb. **Given** always needs a helper.

*Abby **has given** Jessica a talking pencil.*

A **Underline the correct verb in each sentence. Watch for helpers.**

1. Andy (ate eaten) cereal for breakfast.

2. He has (ate eaten) all the grapes.

3. Laura (ate eaten) the bread.

4. The crust was (ate eaten) by the robins.

5. A gray squirrel (ate eaten) the acorn.

B **Underline the correct verb in each sentence. Watch for helpers.**

1. Julio has (gave given) the boys a piece of apple pie.

2. I (gave given) my parakeet some water.

3. A birthday gift was (gave given) by Paul.

4. Some flies were (gave given) to the spider.

5. Olivia (gave given) a loud shout.

Name

Went and *Gone*, *Did* and *Done*

Remember that some verbs need helpers. Some helpers are **has, have, am, is, are, was,** and **were.**

Went is a strong verb. **Gone** is not a strong verb. **Gone** always needs a helper.

> *The mice **have gone** down the hole.*

Did is a strong verb. **Done** is not a strong verb. **Done** always needs a helper.

> *The dishes **were done** before Luis went outside.*

A Write **went** or **gone** to complete each sentence.

1. Danny has _____ to Cartoon World.

2. Julie _____ to New York City.

3. We _____ to the beach.

4. Will has _____ to soccer camp.

5. Tyler was _____ in a flash.

B Underline **did** or **done** to complete each sentence.

1. Beth has (did done) well.

2. We have (did done) the first page.

3. Billy (did done) the painting.

4. The project was (did done) by Regina.

5. Brandon (did done) his work at school.

Name

Am and Is

Some verbs do not show action. These verbs are called **being verbs**.
Am and **is** express being.

Use the being verb **am** with the word **I**.

> **I am** six years old.

Use the being verb **is** when you tell about **one** person,
place, or thing.

> **Lisa is** six years old.

A **Underline the correct verb in each sentence.**

1. The bag of popcorn (is am) on the counter.

2. I (is am) in a new school.

3. The earth (is am) home for many insects.

4. She (is am) the winner of the contest!

B **Complete each sentence with the correct being verb.**

1. I _____ learning about animals.

2. A fox _____ a sly animal.

3. A lion _____ a large cat.

4. I _____ not a fish.

5. An elephant _____ a huge animal.

6. I _____ a mammal.

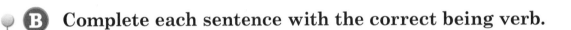

Are

Verbs that do not show action are called being verbs. Some being verbs are **am** and **is**. **Are** is another being verb.

Use the being verb **are** when you tell about **more than one** person, place, or thing.

> *Jon and Anne **are** seven years old.*

Also use **are** with the word **you**.

> *You **are** a funny person.*
> *You **are** good singers.*

Ⓐ **Underline the correct verb in each sentence.**

1. You (is are) my best friend.
2. Candace (am is) the tallest girl in class.
3. They (are am) going to the park.
4. Dean and Adam (are is) twins.
5. I (am are) a fast reader.

Ⓑ **Write your own sentences. Use each being verb below.**

1. **am**

2. **is**

3. **are**

Name _____

Was and Were

Was and **were** are being verbs.

When you write about **one** person, place, or thing, use **was**.

> *Dave **was** outside.*

When you write about **more than one** person, place, or thing, use **were**.

> *Jorge and Matt **were** outside.*

Also use **were** with the word **you**.

> *You **were** late for the game.*

Ⓐ Underline the correct verb in each sentence.

1. Cole (was were) with me.

2. Dawn and Shelby (was were) at the party.

3. The girls (was were) in the pool.

4. The plumber (was were) in the basement.

Ⓑ Complete each sentence with was or were.

1. Many grapes _____ on the vine.

2. Gold _____ in the stream.

3. A million earthworms _____ in the soil.

4. This raisin _____ a grape.

5. A pot of gold _____ at the end of the rainbow.

> Am, is, are, was, and were—
> these are being words.
> When you do not show action,
> you use a being verb.

Watching for Helping Verbs

Remember, some verbs are strong. Some verbs need helping verbs.
Remember to look for **has, have, am, is, are, was,** and **were.**

A Underline **saw** or **seen** to complete each sentence.
Look for helpers.

1. Susan (saw seen) that movie.

2. Jeff has (saw seen) that movie too.

3. Tessa and Amy (saw seen) a play instead.

4. Gretchen has (saw seen) both.

B Underline the correct verb to complete each sentence.
Look for helpers.

1. We have (ate eaten) hot dogs.

2. They (did done) that many times.

3. Jonah (ate eaten) the orange.

4. The men (went gone) to the party.

5. We were (went gone) by five o'clock.

6. Tony (gave give) Tasha the game.

7. The cookies were (did done) in 20 minutes.

8. Will you (gave give) me the basketball?

Name

Watching for Being Verbs

Remember, some verbs can express being. Look for **am, is, are, was,** and **were.**

A Underline the correct verb to complete each sentence.

1. The teacher (was were) glad we won the prize.

2. I (am is) a good swimmer.

3. Many books (is are) in the library.

4. Three boys (was were) in the wagon.

5. The sun (is are) a star.

6. You (is are) always on time.

B Complete each sentence. Use a word from the word bank. Use each word only once.

are	is	was	were	am

1. Kim and Ken _____ twins.

2. Randy _____ happy.

3. Cindy _____ a soccer star.

4. Celia and Aaron _____ at their grandma's house.

5. I _____ taller than my sister.

Name _____

Adverbs

An **adverb** is a word that tells more about a verb.

Some adverbs tell **how** something happens. These words often end in **ly**.

The sun shone brightly.   *The rabbit ran quickly.*
How did the sun shine?   *How did the rabbit run?*
      brightly   **quickly**

Complete each sentence with an adverb from the word bank.

| gently | loudly | neatly | slowly | proudly | carefully |

1. Billy _____ arranged the books on the shelf.

2. Our class yelled _____ at the game.

3. The turtle moved _____ down the road.

4. The team _____ showed their trophy.

5. The breeze blew _____ .

6. Mom let me _____ hold my baby brother.

Writer's Corner

Write your own sentence. Use the adverb *quietly*.

Show What You Know

A Underline the verb in each sentence. If the verb is in the present tense, write **present** on the line. If the verb is in the past tense, write **past** on the line.

1. The boats sailed from the harbor.

2. Carol returned her books to the library.

3. Milla paints a pretty picture.

4. The rain always fills the bucket.

5. We traveled by train across the United States.

B Complete each sentence. Show that something is happening now by adding the letters **ing** to the verb.

1. The children are _____ for the singers. **clap**

2. Tonya is _____ on the lake. **skate**

3. Patty Rabbit is _____ home. **hop**

4. Brian is _____ with my sister. **chat**

5. The water is _____ in the sink. **drip**

Show What You Know

A **Underline the two verbs in each sentence. Then circle the verb that is the helper.**

1. Shannon has gone to the computer lab.

2. The alligators have eaten a tasty dinner.

3. The class is planning a Halloween party.

4. They are going to school.

5. An apple was given to Joely.

B **Underline the correct verb to complete each sentence.**

1. Last week I (see saw) an aardvark.

2. Our class (ate eaten) three pizzas.

3. You (was were) the first one to answer.

4. Martin (has have) a new piano.

5. He (went gone) to the zoo.

6. Andy and Sam (has have) caught many fish.

7. Kristy and Tim (is are) leaving tomorrow.

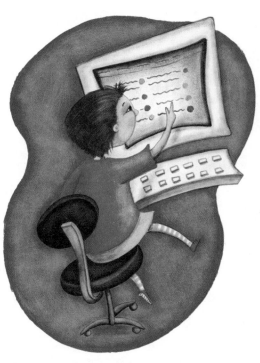

C **Underline the adverb that tells how in each sentence.**

1. The paper wasps' nest is made perfectly.

2. They make a nest carefully.

3. The wasps patiently make the cells of paper.

4. Each row of cells is neatly arranged.

5. I slowly walked away from the nest.

What Is a How-to Article?

Get Ready to Write

You can share how to do things in a how-to article. A how-to article teaches others how to make something or do something.

Title —————— HOW TO MAKE A PAPER SNOWFLAKE

Beginning —————— It's simple to make a paper snowflake.

What You Need list —————— What You Need

white paper   glitter   scissors   glue

Steps to complete the activity —————— Steps

1. First fold your paper two times.
2. Next cut a few shapes around the edge of the paper.
3. Then carefully unfold your paper.
4. Last add glue and a little glitter.

Answer these questions about the how-to article.

1. What is the how-to article about?

2. Where do you learn what the topic is?

3. Where do you find out what you will need?

4. Where do you learn about the steps you need to follow?

Order in a How-to Article

When you give directions, it is important to think about the right order. The words **first**, **next**, **then**, and **last** tell the correct order.

The steps below are not in order. Write the order words First, Next, Then, and Last to tell the correct order.

A _____ stay calm during the fire drill.

_____ go outside.

_____ walk down the hall in a line.

_____ leave the classroom quietly.

B _____ open your eyes.

_____ count to 10.

_____ tag the first person you see.

_____ close your eyes.

First
Next
Then
Last

Steps in a How-to Article

Where does each step belong? Write it on the correct line.

freeze for an hour.	pour juice into the tray.
eat them!	put a craft stick in each cube.

Have you ever made frozen pops? All you need is juice, an ice-cube tray, and craft sticks.

1. **First** _____

2. **Next** _____

3. **Then** _____

4. **Last** _____

put the soil into the cup.	cover the seed with soil.
water it.	press the seed into the soil.

Start your own garden. You need a seed, a cup, some soil, and water.

1. **First** _____

2. **Next** _____

3. **Then** _____

4. **Last** _____

Plan a How-to Article

Think about something you know how to make. Fill in the blanks. Write what you need. Draw a picture of each step.

How to _____

Making _____ is easy and fun.

What You Need

_____   _____

Steps

1. **First**

2. **Next**

3. **Then**

4. **Last**

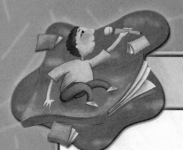

Writer's Workshop

PREWRITING

Pick a Topic

A how-to article tells how to do something or make something. The topic can be anything you know how to make or do.

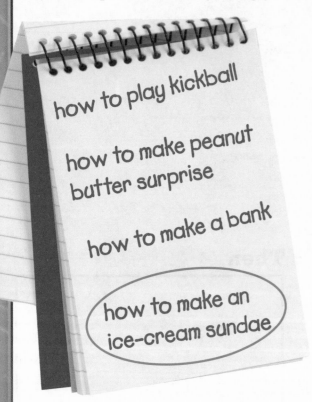

how to play kickball

how to make peanut butter surprise

how to make a bank

how to make an ice-cream sundae

Ben is writing a how-to article. Look at Ben's topic ideas.

List or draw your topic ideas in your notebook. Then think about each idea. Is it something you are an expert at making? Is it something you are a star at doing? Is it something others would like to learn?

Circle the topic you like best. Then write it below.

My topic is:

How to

PREWRITING

Plan Your How-to Article

Now Ben must plan his how-to article. First he writes a What You Need list. Then he writes his steps on separate sentence strips.

WHAT YOU NEED

bowl   whipped cream

ice cream   cherry

chocolate sauce

Steps

put ice cream in bowl

cover with chocolate sauce

put on whipped cream

top with a cherry

Now plan your how-to article. Write a What You Need list in your notebook. Then think about the steps. Think about what your reader needs to know. Write your steps on separate sentence strips or sheets of paper. Then put your steps in the right order.

Writer's Workshop

DRAFTING

This is Ben's draft.

How to Make an Ice-Cream Sundae

Ice-cream sundaes are fun to make and to eat.

What You Need

bowl   whipped cream

ice cream   cherry   chocolate sauce

Steps

1. First put a scoop of ice cream in a bowl.

2. Next covered the ice cream with chocolate sauce.

3. Put on some whipped cream.

4. Last top with a cherry.

Is your mouth watering yet? Go ahead and eat!

Look at your plan. Be sure your sentence strips are in the right order. Add anything that will make your draft clear.

Write your how-to article in your notebook. Use your plan as you write. Include everything you listed in your plan.

To show when something happens, use the words **first**, **next**, **then**, and **last**.

EDITING

Ben uses this Editing Checklist to check his draft.

1. First put a scoop of ice cream in a bowl.

2. Next covered the ice cream with chocolate sauce.
   Then
3. ∧Put on some whipped cream.

I forgot an order word!

Look at the mistake Ben finds. How does he fix it?

Now is the time to make your paper great. Use the Editing Checklist. Try reading your draft aloud. When you find a spot that could be better, mark it on your paper.

REVISING

Ben revises his draft. He writes a new copy. He includes his changes from editing.

Copy your draft. Add anything that will make your draft better. Take out anything that is not helpful.

Writer's Workshop

PROOFREADING

Ben uses this Proofreading Checklist to check his draft.

Proofreading Checklist

☐ Are all the words spelled correctly?

☐ Did I use capital letters?

☐ Did I use the right end marks?

☐ Are all the verbs used correctly?

1. First put a scoop of ice cream in a bowl.
2. Next ~~covered~~ cover the ice cream with chocolate sauce.
3. Then put on some whipped cream.

Look at the mistake that Ben finds. How does he fix it?

Read your how-to article again. Use the checklist to check your draft. Check for one thing at a time. Use the proofreading marks chart at the back of this book. Remember, you can also ask a friend to proofread your draft.

PUBLISHING

Look at how Ben publishes his how-to article. Remember, when you share your work, you are publishing.

Are you ready to share your work? Copy it onto a sheet of paper. Copy your words exactly. Publish the best copy of your work.

You might draw a picture to go with your how-to article. You can draw a picture of the things your reader needs. You can draw a picture of the steps. Or you can draw a picture of what the thing they are doing or making looks like.

Sharing your writing is a great way to show what you know. How will you publish your writing? Decide with your class. Use one of these ideas or one of your own.

Make a poster.

Do a demonstration.

Put in a class How-to Book.

Read it to the class.

Give it to a friend who wants to learn something new.

Pronouns, Adjectives, and Descriptions

Nothing is better than the pond next to my house. All around it are big rocks. I like to dip my feet in the cool water. I love the sweet smell of lilacs. Sometimes Liam and I visit the pond together. We nibble the tangy huckleberries that grow nearby. The frogs and the crickets sound like a crowd of people talking.

Pronouns

A **pronoun** is a word that takes the place of a noun or a group of nouns. Some pronouns you might know are **I, you, they, her, me, he, him, it,** and **us.**

it   he   they   you   we   her

Circle the pronoun in the second sentence that takes the place of the underlined noun or nouns.

1. Ann has the present.   Ann has it.

2. The book is on the shelf.   It is on the shelf.

3. Sue and Rob came to my house.   They came to my house.

4. Tom, saddle the horse.   You saddle the horse.

5. John and I went to the park.   We went to the park.

6. Peggy gave Lynn a gift.   Peggy gave her a gift.

7. Ryan has a small robot.   He has a small robot.

8. Meg's cousins played outside.   They played outside.

9. Brad saw Mike.   He saw Mike.

10. Kim found her trumpet.   Kim found it.

I, me, she, he, it, we, you, and *they—*
these pronouns just might come your way.
They stand in for nouns; they take their place,
like *he* for Jim or *it* for vase.

More Pronouns

Complete each sentence with the correct pronoun. The pronoun should take the place of the underlined noun or nouns.

1. <u>Abby</u> will carry that box.

   _____ will put it on the table.

2. <u>Karen and I</u> are not home.

   _____ are in the pool.

3. Where is <u>my ticket?</u>

   Do you have _____ ?

4. Let's watch <u>Joe</u> practice.

   Do you see _____ ?

5. <u>Jack</u> pitched the ball.

   Did you see how far _____ threw it?

6. Aunt Celine gave <u>Jesse and me</u> the basket.

   She also gave _____ the blanket.

he

She

it

We

us

him

Writer's Corner

Write a sentence about doing something with your best friend. Use the pronoun *we.*

Practice with Pronouns

A pronoun is a word that takes the place of a noun.

Write the correct pronouns to complete these stories.

they	She	It

GOLDILOCKS

Goldilocks went to visit the three bears.

_____ liked the little bear's cereal.

_____ tasted delicious. When

the three bears came home, _____

were surprised to see Goldilocks.

He	him	you	it

THE STUMPY TAIL

Bear wanted to catch some fish. _____ was

very hungry. "I will put my tail in the icy pond,"

he said. When he pulled out his tail, _____

snapped off. What a surprise to _____ !

Were _____ surprised too?

Pronouns Review

A **Write the correct pronoun to complete each sentence.**

1. The book belongs to Caden and Tim.

   Please give it to _____ .

2. Kate is going to the mall.

   May I go with _____ ?

3. Chloe and I like dinosaurs.

   _____ read books about them.

4. Connor and Bailey can sing.

   _____ sang a duet for the show.

5. Kara showed Jacob her computer.

   She let _____ use it.

B **Underline the correct pronoun to complete each sentence.**

1. (She Her) reads adventure books.

2. Ryan bought (she her) a new pencil.

3. Did you put (they them) in the closet?

4. (They Them) are my friends.

5. (He Him) threw the ball.

6. Maggie took (he him) to the zoo.

7. (We Them) are doing our math problems.

8. (Me You) have a sweater like mine.

Pronouns *I* and *Me*

I and **me** are pronouns. Use **I** and **me** when you talk about yourself. Use **I** in the naming part of a sentence. Use **me** in the action part of a sentence.

John and **I** *are friendly.*
I *am friendly.*

The pony is for **me.**
Andy bought tickets for Jeff and **me.**

Read these sentences aloud. Listen for the pronouns I and me. Underline I or me in each sentence. Notice that I is always a capital letter.

1. I want to row the boat.

2. Ally let me try.

3. She watched me row across the lake.

4. My sister and I had a picnic on the shore.

5. Ally let me roast the marshmallows.

More Work with *I* and *Me*

A Write **I** or **me** to complete each sentence.

1. Noah and _____ walked through the forest.

2. _____ found a fossil.

3. He told _____ he'd never seen one.

4. _____ told him it is a print in a stone.

5. Ava and _____ wrote a funny poem.

6. The teacher gave Ava and _____ a prize.

7. Miss Lane told _____ to read it to the class.

8. _____ like to write poems.

B Write your own sentence using the pronoun **I**.

_____

_____

C Write your own sentence using the pronoun **me**.

_____

_____

Name _____

Using *I* in Sentences

Sometimes **I** can be used in the middle of a sentence. This makes a sentence more interesting.

Here is a different way to begin a sentence.

1. Think of a place.

2. Think of what you do there.

3. Make a sentence.

*At home **I** do the dishes.*

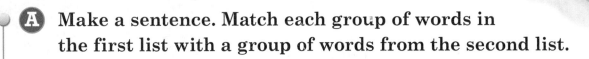

A **Make a sentence. Match each group of words in the first list with a group of words from the second list.**

a place	what I do there
1. At the circus _____	a. I play soccer.
2. In school _____	b. I feed the chickens.
3. On the farm _____	c. I learn to read.
4. On the playground _____	d. I watch the funny clowns.

B **Follow the same directions as above to make more sentences.**

1. At the movies _____	a. I meet many people.
2. At camp _____	b. I eat popcorn.
3. Under the oak tree _____	c. I buy food.
4. In the store _____	d. I rest.

Name

Practice Using *I* in Sentences

Write your own sentences. First think of a place. Use the pictures for help. Then think of what you do there.

1. *In the car*

2. *At the zoo*

3.

4.

5.

Writer's Corner

Write a sentence about a place you go to and what you do there. Use *I* in the middle of the sentence.

Name _____

Pronoun Review

Pronouns are words that take the place of nouns. Some pronouns are about you. Some pronouns are about other people, animals, or things.

A **Write I or me to complete each sentence.**

1. The coach picked _____ for the team.

2. Is the present for _____ ?

3. Brody and _____ met at the door.

4. Ryan, Olivia, and _____ went to the store.

5. Josh lent _____ his bike.

6. May Amelie and _____ go with you?

B **Circle the correct pronoun for the underlined word or words.**

1. Dave and I travel together.   They   We

2. Yue Wan and Jenny are in the pool.   They   We

3. The pencil should be sharpened.   She   It

4. Jacy, ride your bike home.   You   Him

5. I gave Adia a birthday present.   her   she

6. Did Emily give that to Tyler and me? we   us

7. Where is Justin going?   he   him

8. I went with Jose and Maria.   they   them

More Pronoun Review

A Complete each sentence with a pronoun from the word bank. Use each pronoun once.

We	he	him	It	I	me

1. _____ are getting Oscar ready for a race.

2. Sara and _____ gave Oscar some turtle food.

3. _____ is Oscar's favorite snack.

4. Sara takes good care of _____ .

5. She asked _____ to fill his water dish.

6. Sara and I hope _____ is the winner.

B Underline the correct pronoun to complete each sentence.

1. (He Him) got a new watch for his birthday.
2. I wrote (she her) a long letter.
3. Damon watched (they them) play ball.
4. (She Her) plays the radio softly.
5. (It Him) was a sunny afternoon.
6. A spaceship carried (them they) to the moon.
7. Mr. Kovach told (they us) about the eclipse.
8. (We Us) take ballet lessons.

Name _____

Adjectives

An **adjective** tells about a noun. Adjectives describe nouns.
They can tell how something looks, feels, sounds, tastes, or smells.

Ann has **brown** hair.

The baby has **little** toes.

Joe lives in a **big** house.

Use an adjective from the word bank to complete each sentence.

chilly	slow	funny	Red	six	soft

1. The _____ clown made me laugh.

2. _____ leaves fell from the trees.

3. My rabbit has _____ fur.

4. Peter caught _____ fish.

5. It is a _____ day.

6. The _____ turtle lost the race.

An adjective's
a special word
that tells about a noun.
Some adjectives
to describe a shoe
are *big, smelly,* or *brown.*

More Adjectives

Look at the underlined noun in each sentence. Circle the adjective that tells about the noun. The first one is done for you.

1. The (tiny) <u>seal</u> drank milk.

2. The white <u>milk</u> tasted good.

3. The seal fell into the blue <u>water</u>.

4. The little <u>seal</u> swam around.

5. His brown <u>body</u> was a blur.

6. A gray <u>squirrel</u> builds a house.

7. The house is a big <u>nest</u>.

8. The nest is in a small <u>tree</u>.

9. Tasty <u>nuts</u> are hidden in the tree.

10. Don't disturb this busy <u>animal</u>.

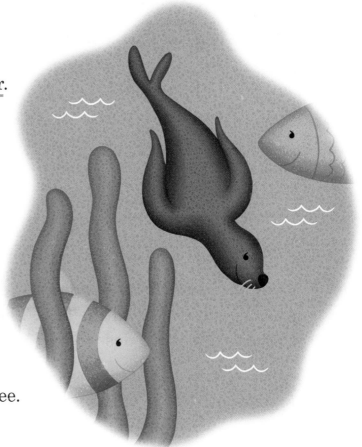

Writer's Corner

Write a sentence about your school. Use an adjective that describes *school*.

Practice with Adjectives

A **Circle the adjective in each sentence. Underline the noun that the adjective describes.**

1. Our town has a shady park.

2. There are old statues in the park.

3. There is a statue of a man with a long beard.

4. The man holds a large book.

5. Another statue is of a giant horse.

6. There are new benches by the horse.

7. The club has long meetings.

8. We will have our spring picnic there.

B **Complete each sentence with the correct adjective. Use the adjectives in the bell. Then underline the noun that the adjective describes.**

1. Kate saw the _____ Liberty Bell.

2. The _____ guide told the bell's history.

3. The _____ visitors asked questions.

4. When it was new, this _____ bell hung in Independence Hall.

5. The _____ bell does not ring anymore.

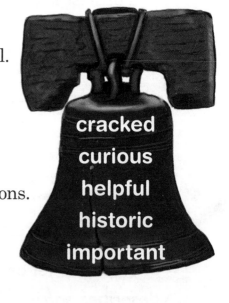

cracked
curious
helpful
historic
important

Sensory Words

People have five senses. They are **sight, sound, smell, taste,** and **touch.**
Some adjectives tell about how things look, sound, smell, taste,
or feel. These adjectives are called **sensory words**.

*We watch the **bright** sunrise.* *I love **buttery** popcorn.*
*I listen to the **loud** cars.* *The puppy has **soft** fur.*
*She wears **sweet** perfume.*

A **Match the sensory words to the thing being described.**

1. sour smoke, orange flame ● ● a. a teakettle
2. bumpy walnuts, sweet chocolate ● ● b. a window
3. sharp thorns, soft petals ● ● c. a campfire
4. whistling noise, white steam ● ● d. a rose
5. dusty curtains, smooth glass ● ● e. a brownie

B **Read the story. Write a sensory word that tells about the
underlined noun. Use the words in the word bank.**

| sweet | Loud | bright | sour | gritty |

The _____ <u>lights</u> swirled around me. The scent of

_____ <u>cotton candy</u> filled the air. _____ <u>voices</u>

chattered everywhere. The _____ <u>sawdust</u> crunched

under my feet. I bit into a _____ <u>pickle</u> and waited

for the show to start.

More Sensory Words

A Circle the sensory word that describes each underlined noun.

1. Deserts are dry <u>areas</u>.

2. Deserts have hot <u>days</u>.

3. Animals in deserts are usually small <u>creatures</u>.

4. Colorful <u>flowers</u> bloom in the desert.

5. That cactus has red <u>flowers</u>.

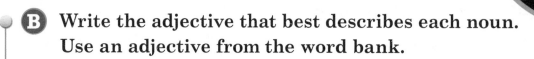

B Write the adjective that best describes each noun. Use an adjective from the word bank.

broken	silly	heavy	loud
pretty	soft	spicy	warm

1. the _____ girl

2. a _____ clown

3. a _____ backpack

4. the _____ window

5. a _____ blanket

6. a _____ coat

7. the _____ music

8. the _____ food

Five senses help us describe the world
we see, we smell, we taste, we touch, we hear.
Use sensory words when you write,
and your description will be loud and clear.

Name

Adjectives That Compare

To compare two people, places, or things, add the letters **er** to an adjective.
To compare three or more people, places, or things, add the letters **est**
to an adjective.

long   long**er**   long**est**

Ⓐ **Underline the adjective in each sentence that ends in er or est.**

1. The sky is brighter today than yesterday.

2. This is the newest flower in the garden.

3. The coolest spot is under the tree.

4. The kitten was slower than the rabbit.

5. Megan is taller than Brent.

Ⓑ **Practice adding the letters er and est to these
adjectives. Write the new words on the lines.**

	er	est
1. fast		
2. cold		
3. hard		
4. short		
5. strong		

More Adjectives That Compare

Some adjectives end in a consonant and have a short vowel sound before the consonant. To make these adjectives compare, double the consonant before adding the letters **er** or **est**.

> *hot*   *hot**ter***   *hot**test***

Some adjectives end in silent **e**. To make these adjectives compare, drop the silent **e** before adding the letters **er** or **est**.

> *cute*   *cut**er***   *cut**est***

A **Make these adjectives compare by doubling the consonant and adding the letters er or est.**

	er	est
1. sad		
2. thin		
3. big		

B **Make these adjectives compare by dropping the e and adding the letters er or est.**

	er	est
1. large		
2. simple		
3. gentle		

> How do you make adjectives that compare? Add -er or -est. These letters help you write about more than two or three.

Name _____

Adjective Review

A **Underline the adjective in each sentence.**

1. A giant tree is near the house.

2. It has rough bark.

3. In autumn it has colorful leaves.

4. The leaves fall on a windy day.

5. It is fun to jump into the biggest pile of leaves.

B **Complete each sentence with a sensory word from the popcorn box.**

1. I ran across the _____ marble floor to the snack stand.

2. The _____ scent of popcorn filled my nose.

3. We got popcorn and _____ candy.

4. We found seats in the _____ theater and waited for the movie to start.

5. When the _____ music began to play, I sat back to enjoy the show!

buttery
smooth
sour
dark
loud

Writer's Corner

Write a sentence with the adjective *softest*. Then write a sentence with the adjective *safer*.

More Adjective Review

A Add the letters **er** and **est** to each adjective. If an adjective ends in a consonant and has a short vowel, double the consonant before adding the letters **er** or **est**. If an adjective ends in silent **e**, drop the silent **e** before adding the letters **er** or **est**.

	er	est
1. thin		
2. great		
3. nice		
4. dark		
5. short		

B Complete each sentence with the correct adjective from the word bank. You will not use all of the adjectives.

tiny	careful	loud	cold	old	bright

1. The _____ moon shone in the sky.

2. Dawn licked a _____ ice-cream cone.

3. The truck made a _____ noise as it stopped.

4. A _____ mouse slid into the hole in the floor.

Name _____

Colorful Poems

You can write your own poems about colors. Here is a poem about the color white.

> *White is the color of*
> *a fluffy cloud,*
> *a wet snowball,*
> *and a scoop of vanilla ice cream.*

A **Finish these poems. Think of things that are each color. The poems do not have to rhyme.**

Yellow is the color of
a shiny ring,
a spoonful of honey,
_____
and _____ .

Red is the color of
a pretty valentine,
_____
a _____ ,
and a screeching fire engine.

B **Write a poem about colors. On the first line, write the name of a color you like. On the next three lines, write three things the color makes you think of. Use adjectives to describe the things.**

_____ is the color of

_____ ,

_____ ,

and _____ .

Show What You Know

A Read the words in the pictures. Color the nouns **red**, the adjectives **blue**, and the pronouns **yellow**.

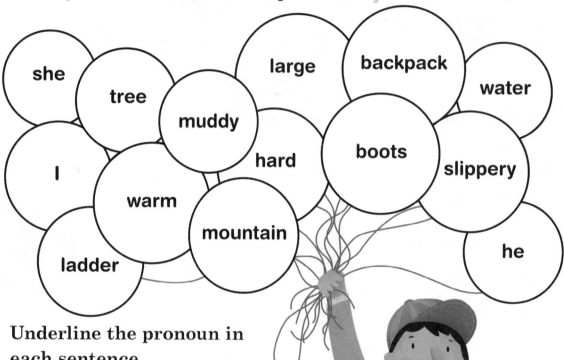

she · tree · large · backpack · water · muddy · I · hard · boots · slippery · warm · mountain · ladder · he

B Underline the pronoun in each sentence.

1. They went to the zoo.

2. The baseball player caught it!

3. Jon saw him climb the ladder.

4. We work hard every day.

5. Dorothy and I are friends.

6. She will be nine years old soon.

7. Please feed them every morning.

8. He wrote a funny story.

9. You climbed over the wall.

10. Joe gave the bats to Susie and me.

Show What You Know

Use a word from the word bank to complete each sentence. Use each word once. Write **a** on the line if the answer is an adjective. Write **p** on the line if the answer is a pronoun.

| you | bright | stormy | Her | smaller |
| five | they | He | biggest | She |

1. _____ name is Jennifer. _____

2. It will be a _____ day. _____

3. _____ is Sean's mother. _____

4. Are _____ coming with me? _____

5. Steve has _____ brothers. _____

6. Joey rode the _____, shiny bike. _____

7. Park School is the _____ school in town. _____

8. _____ went to the store to get milk. _____

9. Did Billy and Julie say where _____ were going? _____

10. Rachel walked with the _____ children. _____

What Is a Description?

Did you ever tell a friend about a new toy? Have you ever told your parents about your day at school? If you did, you gave a description. A **description** tells about a person, a place, a thing, or an event.

I love going to the fair! I visit the mooing cows and clucking chickens. The air smells like piney sawdust. Games and rides light up the night. Sweet cotton candy fills my mouth. My fingers are sticky and pink from my tasty treat.

Answer these questions about the description.

1. What is the description about?

2. Where do you learn what the topic is?

3. What words tell about sight, sound, smell, touch, and taste?

sight

sound

smell

taste

touch

Topic Sentences

A description begins with a topic sentence. The **topic sentence** tells what you are describing. A topic sentence grabs a reader's attention.

Topic Sentence

> *I love to wake up to the sounds and smells of breakfast.* *The smell of bacon tickles my nose. I hear the pop of the toaster and the hiss of spattering butter. Soon I hear eggs cracking against a bowl. I am up before the eggs hit the pan.*

Which is a better topic sentence? Write an X next to the better sentence in each pair.

1. I like lemonade. ☐

   Cold lemonade is perfect on a hot day. ☐

2. My bedroom is nice. ☐

   My bedroom is my favorite place to be. ☐

3. My sister is the cutest baby ever. ☐

   This is what my sister looks like. ☐

4. We have Movie Night every week. ☐

   We watch movies. ☐

Sensory Words

Sensory words paint a picture in a reader's mind. They help the reader imagine the description.

shiny coin   **sight**   *sour* apple   **taste**

barking dogs   **sound**   *hot* sand   **touch**

flowery candle   **smell**

A   **Circle the sensory words in each description. Then draw a line to the sense it uses.**

1. blue sky   ●   ●   sound

2. soft kitten   ●   ●   sight

3. crying baby   ●   ●   smell

4. salty pretzel   ●   ●   taste

5. stinky socks   ●   ●   touch

B   **Fill in each blank with a sensory word from the word bank.**

1. a _____ caterpillar

2. big _____ eyes

3. a _____ winter night

4. my _____ hideout

5. a _____ siren

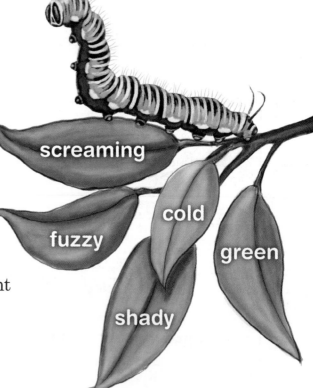

screaming

cold

fuzzy

green

shady

Sensory Words in a Description

A Look at each topic. List three sensory words for each.

recess	a thunderstorm	pizza

B Write one sentence that describes each thing.
Use the sense next to each thing.

1. a fireworks show (**sight**)

2. a farm (**sound**)

3. a campfire (**smell**)

4. hot cocoa (**taste**)

5. tree bark (**touch**)

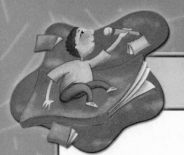

Writer's Workshop

PREWRITING

Pick a Topic

A description tells about a person, a place, a thing, or an event.

my new fish

my friend Liam

the pond near my house

my mom's chicken soup

Maya is writing a description. She lists her topic ideas in her notebook. Then she circles the topic she likes best.

List or draw your topic ideas in your notebook. Your topic can be about a person, a place, a thing, or an event.

Now think about each topic. Is it something you can describe well? Would others like to read about it? Can you think of a good topic sentence? Choose the topic you like best.

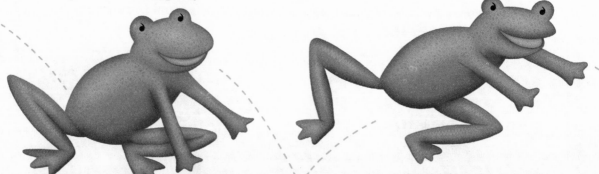

PREWRITING

Plan Your Description

Maya must plan her description. She wants to be sure to add sensory words. She uses a five-senses chart to help her think of ideas. Here is her five-senses chart.

Topic: the pond near my house	
sight	big rocks
sound	frogs and crickets sound like people
smell	lilacs
taste	tangy huckleberries
touch	cool water

Draw in your notebook a five-senses chart like the one Maya used. What sensory words can you think of? Try to write about each of your senses.

Writer's Workshop

DRAFTING

Maya has a lot of sensory words in her five-senses chart. She uses her chart to write her draft. This is Maya's draft.

> Nothing is better than the pond next to my house. All around it are big rocks. I like to dip my feet in the cool water. I love the smell of lilacs. Sometimes Liam and me visit the pond together. We nibble the tangy huckleberries that grow nearby. The frogs and the crickets sound like a crowd of people talking.

Look at the chart you made. Can you think of anything to add? Add any words that will make a better description.

Write your description in your notebook. Begin with a topic sentence that will grab your reader's attention. Use your five-senses chart as you write. Help your readers see, smell, hear, taste, and feel what you describe.

EDITING

Maya wants to make her draft great. She reads her draft. She uses this Editing Checklist for help.

> sweet
> I love the ∧smell of lilacs. Sometimes
>
> Liam and me visit the pond together.
>
> We nibble the tangy huckleberries that

Look at the mistake that Maya finds. How does she fix it?

Read your draft. See if you can answer yes to the questions on the Editing Checklist. Mark any parts that could be better. Help your readers see, smell, hear, taste, and feel what you describe.

I forgot a sensory word!

REVISING

After Maya edits her draft, she revises it. She fixes the mistake she marked. She copies her draft on a sheet of paper.

Copy your draft. Make your description better than it was before. Fix any mistakes you marked.

Writer's Workshop

PROOFREADING

Maya proofreads her description. She looks at this Proofreading Checklist as she reads. She marks her paper where she wants it to be better.

Proofreading Checklist

☐ Are all the words spelled correctly?

☐ Did I use capital letters?

☐ Did I use the right end marks?

☐ Are pronouns and adjectives used correctly?

I love the sweet smell of lilacs. Sometimes
                    I
Liam and ∧me visit the pond together.

We nibble the tangy huckleberries that

Look at the mistake Maya finds. How does she fix it?

Read your description again. Check the Proofreading Checklist as you read. Put an **X** next to the question if you can answer yes. You might ask a partner to proofread your paper. Have your partner use the checklist.

Fix any mistakes you see. Use the proofreading marks chart on the inside back cover of your book. Mark your corrections on your paper.

PUBLISHING

When you publish, you share your work with others. Maya is almost ready to publish. She carefully copies her description onto a sheet of paper. Maya wants to share her very best work. She publishes by putting her description on a bulletin board.

Copy your description. Write as neatly as you can. You might type it on a computer instead.

How will you publish your description? Decide with your class. Use one of these ideas or one of your own.

Frame it.

Hang it up.

Put it on a bulletin board.

Read it to the class.

Make a class book of Descriptions.

Contractions and Book Reports

Quotation Station

Reading is to the
mind what exercise
is to the body.

—*Joseph Addison*
author

Lion

Zebras

Elephants

A Great Book!

by Julio Arroyo Covas

Louise Fatio wrote the book <u>The Happy Lion</u>. The Happy Lion lives at a zoo in France. Every day friends come by to visit him. His friends are Francois, Monsieur Dupont, and Madame Pinson. One day the lion sees that his cage is open. So the lion decides to return his friends' visits. When his friends see him, they run away. The Happy Lion can't figure out why. I think this book is great because of the lion. No matter what happens, he's a happy lion!

Contractions

A **contraction** is a short way of writing two words. When you write a contraction, you leave out a letter or letters and put in an **apostrophe**. This is an apostrophe (').

Some contractions are made using the word **not**. When you make a contraction with **not**, drop the **o** and put in an apostrophe.

A **Trace over the contractions below.**

do not	have not	has not	did not
don't	*haven't*	*hasn't*	*didn't*

B **Write the contraction for the two underlined words.**

1. I <u>do not</u> have a hole in my pocket.

2. Matt <u>has not</u> put the puzzle together.

3. The birds <u>have not</u> flown south yet.

4. Leslie <u>did not</u> plant the seeds correctly.

5. Tomas <u>has not</u> made his bed today.

6. They <u>have not</u> been to the museum.

7. I <u>do not</u> want to go to the mall.

8. We <u>did not</u> have time to fly the kites.

Name _____

Contractions Practice

A **Underline the contraction that is spelled correctly to complete each sentence.**

1. Jorge (didn't did'nt) find his skates.

2. My brother and I (do'nt don't) stay up late.

3. Chris (hasn't has'nt) read that book.

4. The rabbits (haven't have'nt) eaten the carrots and lettuce.

5. Paul (didn't did'nt) finish the math problems.

B **Complete each sentence with a contraction on the right. You will use some contractions twice.**

1. Deshan _____ done his homework.

2. I _____ want to play in the snow.

3. My sister _____ pack my lunch.

4. The trees _____ shed their leaves yet.

5. This apple _____ been eaten.

don't

hasn't

haven't

didn't

Writer's Corner

Write a sentence about a food you do not like.
Use the contraction *don't*.

Name _____

More Contractions with *Not*

Remember that some contractions are made with the word **not**.
Here are more contractions that are made with the word **not**.

A Trace over the contractions below.

could not	are not	does not	is not
couldn't	*aren't*	*doesn't*	*isn't*

B Write the contraction for the two underlined words.

1. Molly <u>does not</u> take piano lessons.

2. Those explorers <u>are not</u> giving up.

3. The sun <u>is not</u> seen at night.

4. A worm <u>does not</u> have bones.

5. The birds <u>are not</u> flying too close.

6. Bryan <u>could not</u> tie his shoes.

7. The river <u>is not</u> very deep.

8. The train <u>could not</u> move on the track.

Name _____

Writing Contractions with *Not*

Complete each sentence with a contraction. Use a word from the lily pads. You will use some contractions twice.

1. The lions _____ in the cage.

2. A toad _____ have smooth skin.

3. An egg _____ square.

4. The fox _____ catch the rabbits.

5. This cow _____ have horns.

6. Wild animals _____ friendly.

7. I _____ pet the lion at the zoo.

8. That pickle _____ sweet.

9. The bell _____ ring on time.

10. The fish _____ been fed today.

couldn't
didn't
aren't
haven't
isn't
doesn't

Name _____

Working with Contractions

Some contractions are made using the word **not**. Here are more contractions made using the word **not**.

A Trace over the contractions below.

was not *wasn't*

were not *weren't*

cannot *can't*

will not *won't*

B Write the contraction for the underlined words.

1. The gorillas <u>were not</u> fed yet. _____

2. Rory <u>was not</u> in the three-legged race. _____

3. Jason <u>cannot</u> keep the squirrel as a pet. _____

4. A scout <u>will not</u> play with matches. _____

5. The horses <u>were not</u> wild. _____

6. It <u>was not</u> too cold to play outside. _____

7. I <u>will not</u> eat peanut butter and pickles. _____

8. She <u>cannot</u> mix the paint. _____

Name _____

More Working with Contractions

Underline the contraction that is spelled correctly in each sentence.

1. The train (wasn't was'nt) at the station.

2. Kerry (wo'nt won't) skip rope with me.

3. Dogs (can't ca'nt) climb trees.

4. The deer (won't wo'nt) eat the leaves.

5. The birds (were'nt weren't) flying today.

6. (Wasn't Was'nt) your birthday last week?

7. I (ca'nt can't) catch the butterfly.

8. Flowers (won't wo'nt) grow without water.

9. (Can't Ca'nt) Terry play the game?

10. It (was'nt wasn't) a good day for a picnic.

A contraction is a way
to write two words as one.
Replace a letter or letters with an apostrophe,
and it's already done.

Writer's Corner

Write a sentence about a place you will not go.
Use the contraction *won't*.

Contractions with *Not* Review

A contraction is a short way of writing two words. When you write a contraction, you leave out a letter or letters and put in an apostrophe.

Ⓐ Write the correct contraction for each set of words.

do not		will not	
cannot		did not	
has not		have not	
were not		are not	
could not		does not	
is not		was not	

Ⓑ Write the two words that make up each underlined contraction.

1. The boys <u>don't</u> have a game today.

2. This window <u>won't</u> open.

3. A queen bee <u>doesn't</u> do any work.

4. The rooster <u>didn't</u> crow on time.

5. Her goldfish <u>weren't</u> in the pond.

6. We <u>haven't</u> opened the presents yet.

More Contractions with *Not* Review

A Write the contraction for the two words in blue.

1. I _____ write a poem about trees.   **could not**

2. Sue _____ given Dad the mail.   **has not**

3. A fir tree _____ have leaves.   **does not**

4. Emil _____ search for frogs.   **will not**

5. Turtles _____ very fast.   **are not**

6. The apples _____ ripened.   **have not**

7. Pepper _____ wearing a collar.   **is not**

8. Our old house _____ very big.   **was not**

B Write a sentence using the contraction **doesn't**.

_____

_____

_____

C Write a sentence using the contraction **isn't**.

_____

_____

_____

_____

Contractions with *Am* and *Is*

Some contractions are made with the word **am**. When you make a contraction with **am**, use an apostrophe in place of the **a**.

A Trace over the contraction below.

I am   *I'm*

Some contractions are made with the word **is**. When you make a contraction with **is**, use an apostrophe in place of the **i**.

B Trace over the contractions below.

he is	she is	it is
he's	*she's*	*it's*

C Write the contraction for the two underlined words.

1. I am going to New York City.

2. He is my favorite author.

3. It is time to walk the dog.

4. She is running in a race.

5. I am seven years old today.

Name _____

Contractions with *Are*

Some contractions are made with the word **are**. When you make a contraction with **are**, use an apostrophe in place of the **a**.

A Trace over the contractions below.

you are	we are	they are
you're	*we're*	*they're*

B Write the two words that make up each contraction.

we're	you're	they're
_____	_____	_____

C Underline the contraction that is spelled correctly in each sentence.

1. I know (you're yo'ure) going to camp.
2. (Wer'e We're) going to camp too.
3. (They're The'yre) not going with us.
4. (Yo'ure You're) going to be in Cabin A?
5. (We're Wer'e) in Cabin B!

Contractions with *Am*, *Is*, and *Are*

A Look at the words below. Put the words together to make contractions. You will use some words more than once. Write the contractions on the lines.

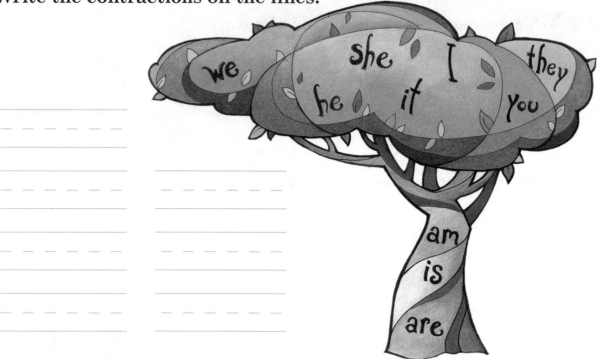

B Write the contraction for the two underlined words.

1. <u>You are</u> going to make a cake.

2. Do you think <u>he is</u> coming to town?

3. <u>They are</u> going with Emily.

4. Grace thinks <u>it is</u> a hard song.

5. I know <u>we are</u> going to like the play.

6. <u>She is</u> not coming home.

Name _____

Contractions with *Have*

Some contractions are made with the word **have.** When you make a contraction with **have**, use an apostrophe in place of the **ha**.

A Trace over the contractions below.

I have	you have	we have	they have
I've	you've	we've	they've

B Write the contraction for the two underlined words.

1. I <u>have</u> been at the swimming pool.

2. Do you think <u>we have</u> bought too many cookies?

3. <u>You have</u> got mustard on your shirt.

4. I think <u>they have</u> got enough balloons.

5. <u>We have</u> done a lot of painting today.

6. Did you hear about what <u>I have</u> won?

7. <u>They have</u> told us to bring cake.

8. I think <u>we have</u> put up too many streamers.

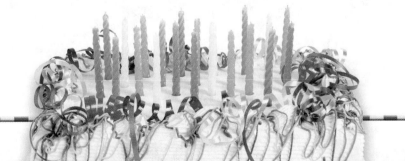

Contractions with *Has*

Some contractions are made with the word **has**. When you make a contraction with **has**, use an apostrophe in place of the **ha**.

A Trace over the contractions below.

he has	she has	it has
he's	*she's*	*it's*

B Write in each sentence the contraction for the blue words.

1. I think _____ gone to the store.   **he has**

2. _____ been a long day.   **It has**

3. Petra says _____ forgotten the letter.   **she has**

4. I think _____ got a swimming pool.   **she has**

5. _____ never been broken.   **It has**

6. _____ stopped at Marc's house.   **He has**

Contractions with *Have* and *Has*

A Draw a line from the words in the first list
to their contractions in the second list.

1. I have   ●   ● they've

2. he has   ●   ● it's

3. it has   ●   ● we've

4. they have   ●   ● she's

5. you have   ●   ● he's

6. she has   ●   ● you've

7. we have   ●   ● I've

B Write each sentence. Write a contraction
for the underlined words in each sentence.

1. I have got a parakeet.

2. Do you know where they have been?

3. I think she has gone home.

4. He has been at Cary's house.

5. I think you have stayed up too late.

Name

Reviewing Contractions

A Write the contraction for each set of words.

it is _____   you have _____

they have _____   it has _____

I am _____   we are _____

we have _____   he is _____

you are _____   they are _____

she is _____   she has _____

he has _____   I have _____

B Underline the contraction in each sentence. Then
write the two words that make up the contraction.

1. It's for my teacher. _____

2. I think I've got a dollar. _____

3. Cara thinks she's a good pitcher. _____

4. We're going to ride the Zapper. _____

5. I'm tall enough to ride it. _____

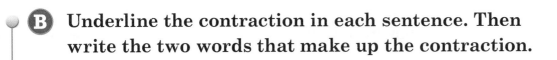

More Reviewing Contractions

Write in each sentence the contraction for the two blue words.

1. *It's* _____ a pretty day.   **It is**

2. Dad said that _____ going to work.   **he is**

3. Rachel said _____ going swimming.   **she is**

4. _____ making a sandcastle.   **I am**

5. _____ going to watch me.   **They are**

6. I think _____ stopped raining.   **it has**

7. _____ lived here for 20 years.   **They have**

8. I think _____ met your sister.   **I have**

9. _____ flown to Egypt twice.   **We have**

10. _____ been to the zoo?   **You have**

11. _____ having a party.   **We are**

12. _____ joking!   **You are**

Contractions with *Had*

Some contractions are made with the word **had.** When you make a contraction with **had,** use an apostrophe in place of the **ha.**

A **Draw a line from the words in the first list to their contractions in the second list.**

1. he had ●   ● she'd

2. I had ●   ● I'd

3. she had ●   ● he'd

B **Write the contraction for the blue words.**

1. _____ better get here on time. **She had**

2. I knew _____ gotten a new bike. **he had**

3. _____ eaten two apples. **I had**

4. I think _____ shut off the light. **she had**

5. Mom said _____ slept too long. **I had**

6. _____ given me the garden hose. **He had**

Writer's Corner

Write a sentence about a member of your family. Use the contraction *he'd* or *she'd.*

Name _____

More Contractions with *Had*

Some contractions are made with the word **had**. When you make a contraction with **had**, an apostrophe takes the place of the **ha**.

Ⓐ **Trace over the contractions below.**

you had	we had	they had
you'd	*we'd*	*they'd*

Ⓑ **Write the two words that make up the underlined contraction in each sentence.**

1. Alena said <u>they'd</u> been to the movie theater. _____

2. Jared wondered where <u>you'd</u> been. _____

3. I wish <u>we'd</u> taken a blanket. _____

4. <u>You'd</u> better do your homework. _____

5. <u>They'd</u> been on a long plane ride. _____

6. <u>We'd</u> won a prize. _____

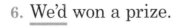

Show What You Know

A **Draw a line from each contraction to the word or words that make up the contraction.**

1. couldn't ● ● will not

2. I've ● ● did not

3. won't ● ● cannot

4. didn't ● ● could not

5. can't ● ● I have

1. hasn't ● ● they had

2. didn't ● ● I am

3. I'm ● ● did not

4. I'd ● ● I had

5. they'd ● ● has not

1. we'd ● ● you are

2. we're ● ● we have

3. they're ● ● we had

4. you're ● ● we are

5. we've ● ● they are

B **Underline the correct contraction to complete each sentence.**

1. Brady (haven't couldn't) find his gloves.

2. Melody (wasn't weren't) playing in the sun.

3. (I've I'm) gotten a new raincoat.

4. During the thunderstorm, the team (hasn't didn't) play ball.

Show What You Know

A **Underline the contraction in each sentence. Then write the word or words that make up the contraction.**

1. The peanuts weren't for the elephants.

2. I think I've discovered a new planet!

3. The octopus won't come out of its home.

4. I'm ready to put the bait on my hook.

5. We can't see the moon tonight.

B **Write each sentence. Write a contraction for the underlined words.**

1. The whale watchers have not seen a whale.

2. You do not have the right time.

3. I am ready to enter the spaceship.

What Is a Book Report?

Get Ready to Write

Have you ever read a book that you really liked? Have you ever read a book that wasn't very good? In a book report you tell about a book you have read. You share

the **title**—the name of the book. Underline the title of the book.

the **author**—the person who wrote the book.

the **characters**—the people or things in the book.

your **opinion**—how you felt or what you thought about the book.

Title — Aunt Eater's Mystery Vacation is by Doug Cushman. — **Author**

The book is about Aunt Eater. Aunt Eater takes a — **Character**

vacation to rest and read mystery books. But she

ends up in a real mystery! I like this book because

Opinion — Aunt Eater is smart and she likes mysteries.

Answer these questions about the book report.

1. What is the title of the book?

2. Who is the author of the book?

3. Who are the characters?

4. How does the writer feel about this book?

Parts of a Book Report

A good book report has a **beginning**, a **middle**, and an **ending**.

The **beginning** tells the title and the author's name. It also tells who the characters are. Remember to underline the title.

The **middle** tells what happens in the book.

The **ending** tells how you feel or what you thought about the book.

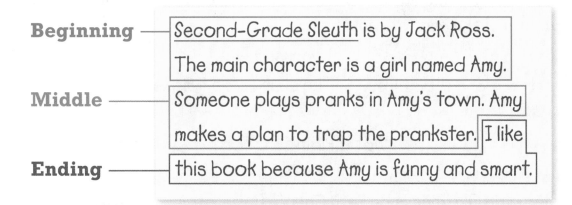

Beginning — <u>Second-Grade Sleuth</u> is by Jack Ross. The main character is a girl named Amy.

Middle — Someone plays pranks in Amy's town. Amy makes a plan to trap the prankster. I like

Ending — this book because Amy is funny and smart.

The parts of a book report are all mixed up. Write the correct number in each box to put the report in order.

1. beginning   2. middle   3. ending

☐ This book is great because it shows that we are all special.

☐ <u>Why Can't I Fly?</u> is by Ken Brown. It's about Cecil the Ostrich.

☐ Cecil can't fly like other birds. But he finds out he has his own special talent.

Opinions in Book Reports

Your **opinion** is how you feel or what you think about a book. Tell your opinion of the book in the ending. Explain why you feel the way you do.

First tell your opinion. Here are some opinions you might have about a book.

I like this book.   I thought the book would be better.

I didn't like this book.   Everyone should read this book.

Then tell why you have the opinion you do. Here are some reasons why you might feel the way you do.

The story was funny.   I guessed what would happen right away.

The book has great pictures.   The story didn't make sense.

> Not a Plain Old Story
> by Lee Martin
>
> Just a Plain Old Tree is by Beth Chung. It is a story about Zena and Rudi. On a walk they hear a noise coming from a hole in a tree. They crawl inside to investigate. Zena and Rudi find themselves in a magical place full of flying animals that act like people. This book is great! The pictures are good. The story makes you laugh.

1. What is Lee's opinion of this book?

_____

_____

2. Why does Lee feel the way he does?

_____

_____

_____

Organize a Book Report

A chart can help you organize a book report. A chart can help make sure you don't forget any parts.

Pick a book you have read. Fill in the chart below. The first, last, and important words in a book title should begin with capital letters. Remember to underline the title.

Beginning	Title	
	Author	
	Characters	
Middle	What happens	
Ending	How I felt about the book and why	

Writer's Workshop

PREWRITING

Pick a Topic

Julio is writing a book report. First he needs to pick a topic. Julio thinks about the books that he's read. He lists them in his notebook. Then he circles <u>The Happy Lion</u>. He thinks his classmates would enjoy hearing about this book the most.

Diary of a Worm

The Giving Tree

Henry and Mudge in the Sparkle Days

If You Give a Pig a Party

The Happy Lion

Make a list of books you have read. Then think about each book. Do you remember the book well? Would you enjoy writing about it? Would others enjoy reading it? Pick the book you will write about. Circle the title.

PREWRITING

Plan Your Book Report

Julio needs to plan his book report. He knows that if he makes a plan first, his report will be easier to write. Here is the plan Julio makes.

Beginning	Title	The Happy Lion
	Author	Louise Fatio
	Characters	The Happy Lion, Francois, Monsieur Dupont, Madame Pinson
Middle	What happens	The Happy Lion's friends visit him. The lion goes out to visit friends. People are scared of the lion.
Ending	How I felt about the book and why	I liked this book. No matter what, the lion is always happy.

Make a plan for your book report. Draw a chart like Julio's in your notebook. Make sure you include the **beginning**, the **middle**, and the **ending**. Fill in all the information. Read the book again if you need to.

Writer's Workshop

DRAFTING

Julio has a lot of information in his chart. He uses his chart to write his draft. Julio is careful to follow his plan.

> *A Great Book!*
>
> *by Julio Arroyo Covas*
>
> *Louise Fatio wrote the book The Happy Lion. The Happy Lion lives at a zoo in France. Every day friends come by to visit him. His friends are Francois, Monsieur Dupont, and Madame Pinson. One day the lion sees that his cage is open. So the lion decides to return his friends' visits. When his friends see him, they run away. The Happy Lion ca'nt figure out why. I think this book is great because of the lion.*

Write your draft in your notebook. Use your plan as you write. Read your book again if you need to. Add anything to your book report that will make it great. Remember that you'll have time to make changes later.

EDITING

Julio edits his report to make it better. He uses this checklist. He checks for one question at a time.

they run away. The Happy Lion ca'nt figure out why. I think this book is great because of the lion. ∧No matter what happens, he's a happy lion!

Look at the mistake Julio finds. How does he fix it?

Edit your book report. Use the checklist that Julio used. Make any changes that will make your draft better.

Read aloud your book report. How does it sound? How can you make it better?

My ending doesn't tell why I have my opinion.

REVISING

Julio revises his draft. He fixes the mistake he marked. He copies it onto a sheet of paper.

Copy your draft. Fix any mistakes you marked. Make sure you can answer yes to all the questions on the checklist.

Writer's Workshop

PROOFREADING

Julio proofreads his book report. By proofreading he will catch even more mistakes.

Julio uses a proofreading checklist. He reads his paper carefully. He looks at one question at a time.

Proofreading Checklist

☐ Are all the words spelled correctly?

☐ Did I use capital letters?

☐ Did I use the right end marks?

☐ Are contractions used correctly?

return his friends' visits. When his friends see him, they run away. The Happy Lion ca'nt figure out why.
can't

Look at the mistake Julio finds. How does he fix it?

Proofread your paper. Use the Proofreading Checklist. If you have trouble checking a mistake, ask a friend or your teacher for help. Make your book report one that others will enjoy reading.

PUBLISHING

When you publish you share your book report with others. Julio is excited to publish his book report. He wants other people to read <u>The Happy Lion</u>. Julio makes a clean copy of his book report. Then he makes a poster for the book and puts it with his report.

Copy your book report onto a sheet of paper. Add a title for your book report. Maybe someone will read your book report and want to read the book you chose!

Decide how to publish your book report. Here are some ways you might publish. Can you think of other ways?

Put your book report on the class bulletin board.

Pretend you are selling the book on TV.

Put all the book reports in a class magazine.

Draw an ad for your book. Attach it to your book report.

Word Study and Research Reports

An Enormous Animal

The blue whale is the largest animal on Earth. It lives in the sea. Some blue whales weigh 200 tons. A blue whale's tongue can weigh as much as an elephant. A blue whale's food is called krill. Krill are very tiny animals that are like shrimp. Blue whales can eat 12,000 pounds of krill a day. The blue whale is the largest animal, but it eats some of the smallest food.

Synonyms

Synonyms are words that have the same or almost the same meaning. Use a synonym instead of using the same word over and over.

Be **quiet**.
Be **silent**.

Did you **talk** to me about that?
Did you **speak** to me about that?

Andy is **afraid** of the elephant.
Andy is **scared** of the elephant.

The squirrel will **find** the nut.
The squirrel will **discover** the nut.

Did the cat **hurt** the mouse?
Did the cat **harm** the mouse?

James started to **pull** the wagon.
James started to **tug** the wagon.

When can you **begin**?
When can you **start**?

It's **hard** to turn this doorknob.
It's **difficult** to turn this doorknob.

Write a synonym for each word. Use the examples above.

1. discover _____

2. talk _____

3. start _____

4. silent _____

5. tug _____

6. hard _____

7. harm _____

8. afraid _____

Synonyms, synonyms, we know quite a few.
Quick and *fast, shout* and *yell, glad* and *happy* too.
Synonyms, synonyms, how our list will grow.
Words that we call synonyms are jolly friends to know.

Synonym Practice

Read each sentence. Write a synonym for the underlined word. Use the words on the right for help.

1. Justin will <u>pull</u> the heavy wagon.

   Justin will _____ the heavy wagon.

2. Are you <u>scared</u> of storms?

   Are you _____ of storms?

3. The audience was <u>silent</u>.

   The audience was _____ .

4. <u>Begin</u> the race now.

   _____ the race now.

5. Please <u>talk</u> about your trip.

   Please _____ about your trip.

6. Did Logan <u>find</u> the diamond?

   Did Logan _____ the diamond?

7. Be sure you don't <u>harm</u> the grass.

   Be sure you don't _____ the grass.

8. The math problem was <u>hard</u>.

   The math problem was _____ .

hurt

tug

discover

afraid

difficult

quiet

Start

speak

More Synonyms

A Read the words in the balls. Color each pair of synonyms the same color.

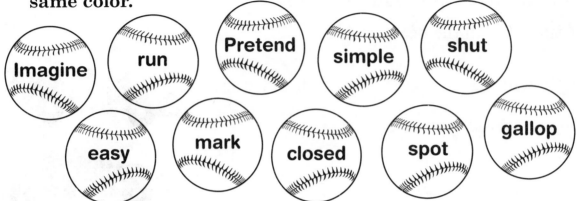

B Rewrite each sentence using a synonym in place of the underlined word.

1. I erased the mark on my paper.

2. The directions were easy to follow.

3. The wind closed the door.

4. The horse will run across the field.

5. Pretend that you have three wishes.

Name _____

More Synonym Practice

A Look at the words. Write on the line a synonym for each word.

easy _____

imagine _____

shut _____

spot _____

run _____

B Read each sentence. Circle the correct synonym for the underlined word.

1. This recipe is simple. (hard easy)

2. Did you clean that mark off of the floor? (spot paper)

3. I like to imagine that I am an actor. (worry pretend)

4. We might gallop like horses in gym today. (run hop)

5. Leah closed the cupboard. (shut opened)

Writer's Corner

Write two sentences about two things you do well.
Use *easy* in one sentence. Use *simple* in the other sentence.

Name _____

Working with Synonyms

A Read the words in the hearts. Color each pair of synonyms the same color.

B Rewrite each sentence. Use a synonym in place of the underlined word.

1. My <u>pal</u> and I work together.

   _____

2. We fold a <u>large</u> sheet of paper.

   _____

3. Then we glue on <u>small</u> yellow stars.

   _____

4. Our teacher will be <u>glad</u> to see the card we made.

   _____

Synonyms Review

A Read the pairs of words. Write **yes** if the pairs are synonyms. Write **no** if the pairs are not synonyms.

1. find   discover _____   4. closed   shut _____

2. easy   big _____   5. pull   little _____

3. talk   simple _____   6. hurt   harm _____

B Draw a line from each word in the first list to its synonym in the second list.

1. quiet   ●   ● imagine

2. mark   ●   ● friend

3. pal   ●   ● happy

4. hard   ●   ● spot

5. pretend ●   ● silent

6. glad   ●   ● difficult

Writer's Corner

Write two sentences about two things in your bedroom.
Use *large* in one sentence. Use *big* in the other sentence.

Antonyms

Antonyms are words that have opposite meanings.

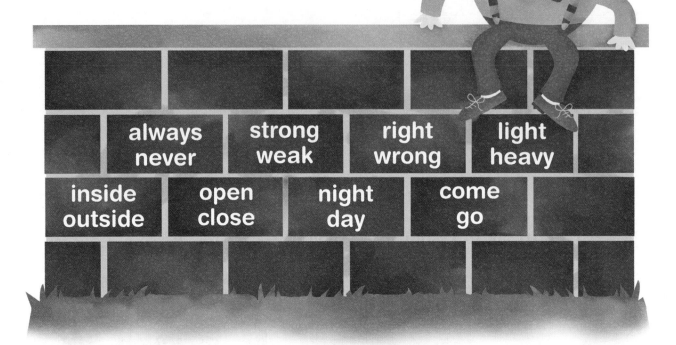

always
never

strong
weak

right
wrong

light
heavy

inside
outside

open
close

night
day

come
go

○ **Read each sentence aloud. Write the antonym of the underlined word. Use the words in the bricks for help.**

1. The answer is right. _____

2. Please take the cat outside. _____

3. I always eat peanut butter. _____

4. My bookbag is heavy. _____

5. That was a strong rope. _____

Name

More Antonyms

Write each sentence. Replace the underlined word with its antonym. Use the word bank if you need help.

| heavy | go | open | day | never |

1. Please close the door.

2. The party lasted all night.

3. This book is light.

4. I always clean my room.

5. Can Belle come too?

Writer's Corner

Write two sentences about things you have to do. Use the antonyms *night* and *day*.

Name _____

Antonym Practice

Here are some more antonyms.

up
down

sad
happy

over
under

small
large

short
tall

high
low

far
near

thick
thin

Complete each sentence with the antonym of the underlined word. Use the words above if you need help.

1. Tara lives <u>near</u> us, but Cole lives _____ from us.

2. A kitten is <u>small</u>, but a lion is _____ .

3. Chloe sings <u>high</u>, but Hope sings _____ .

4. This pole is <u>thin</u>, but that one is _____ .

5. Lee is <u>happy</u> today, but his sister is _____ .

6. Julie is going <u>up</u> the stairs, but Daniel is going _____ .

7. My cousin is <u>tall</u>, but I am _____ .

8. The rabbit hopped <u>under</u> the bush, but the bird flew _____ it.

Working with Antonyms

Look at each set of pictures. Write the correct word for each picture. Use the antonym pairs below for help.

full	fast	stop	dry	cold	first
empty	slow	go	wet	hot	last

1.

_____

2.

_____

3.

_____

4.

_____

5.

_____

6.

_____

Antonyms Review

A **Match each question with the correct answer. Then underline the antonyms in each question and answer.**

1. Is a turtle <u>fast</u>?   ●   ● No, he is last in line.

2. Was the jar full?   ●   ● No, it is <u>slow</u>.

3. Is Peter first in line?   ●   ● No, it is cold.

4. Is the dog's nose hot?   ●   ● No, it was empty.

5. Does a green light mean stop? ●   ● No, it is dry.

6. Is the sidewalk wet?   ●   ● No, it means go.

B **Match each word in the first list to its antonym in the second list.**

1. light   ●   ● empty

2. sad   ●   ● never

3. full   ●   ● under

4. always ●   ● heavy

5. over   ●   ● happy

1. inside   ●   ● thin

2. thick   ●   ● last

3. fast   ●   ● outside

4. come   ●   ● go

5. first   ●   ● slow

Synonyms and Antonyms Review

A Read each sentence. Circle the correct synonym for the underlined word.

1. Andy is afraid of alligators. (scared glad)

2. Jeff is a silent boy. (quiet loud)

3. Leslie is my best pal. (enemy friend)

4. That math problem is simple. (easy hard)

5. Sam likes to imagine that he is a basketball player. (start pretend)

6. Eric closed the comic book. (opened shut)

B Read each sentence. Write an antonym for the underlined word.

1. My brother thinks he is always right. _____

2. Your uncle is short. _____

3. It is cold today. _____

4. I always wear my hair this way. _____

Name _____

Homophones

Homophones are words that sound alike but are spelled differently and have different meanings. Look at these homophones.

*I thought I **knew** the answer.*
*This shirt is **new.***

Our car is in the driveway.
*The clock is an **hour** fast.*

*Do you want to **buy** it?*
*Did the train pass **by**?*

*Did you **meet** my cousin?*
*There is **meat** on this sandwich.*

Underline the correct homophone in each sentence.

1. The bus is one (our <u>hour</u>) late.

2. Is your bike (knew new)?

3. Dad drove (by buy) the parade.

4. Do lions eat (meet meat)?

5. Anita will (buy by) the lemons.

6. Carlos (new knew) his street address.

7. I got to (meet meat) my favorite actor!

8. (Hour Our) science experiment was fun.

Writer's Corner

Write two sentences about the grocery store. Use *buy* in one sentence. Use *by* in the other sentence.

Homophone Practice

A Write the correct word in each blank.

meat

hour   buy

1. Jacob _____ he would get a _____ bike.

by   new

2. _____ party starts in one _____ .

meet   Our

3. Stop _____ the store and _____ some milk.

knew

4. Did you _____ the man who doesn't eat _____ ?

B Read each sentence. If the underlined homophone is correct, put an **X** on the line. If the homophone is not correct, write the correct homophone on the line.

1. Did Shelby <u>meat</u> Josh? _____

2. Can Marissa come to <u>our</u> house? _____

3. Anthony wants to <u>buy</u> that game. _____

4. Is that the <u>knew</u> book? _____

5. Did Melanie come <u>buy</u> the house? _____

6. Your watch is one <u>hour</u> slow. _____

7. I <u>knew</u> that you had my book! _____

More Homophones

Here are some more homophones.

Lily is reading a fairy **tale**.　　It is **eight** o'clock.

The squirrel has a bushy **tail**.　　Ryan **ate** his breakfast.

Here is your birthday cake.　　Will you **be** at Ethan's party?

Did you **hear** the bird?　　Erin was stung by a **bee**.

A Underline the correct homophone in each sentence.

1. Did you (hear here) the jet roar?

2. Jada told us a fairy (tail tale).

3. Tyler (ate eight) Chinese food.

4. (Hear Here) is the hidden treasure!

5. The bear's (tail tale) is short.

6. (Ate Eight) pencils rolled off the desk.

B Underline the homophone pair in each sentence.

1. Stand here until you hear the bell ring.

2. Dylan ate eight pieces of candy.

3. We listened to a tale about a peacock's colorful tail.

4. That bee will be going back to its hive.

Working with Homophones

You will probably use these homophones when you write.

*Can you **see** the board?*   *Look at the baby **deer**!*

*This ship sails the **sea**.*   *Kara is a **dear** little girl.*

*What did you **write** about?*   *My arm was **weak** after I broke it.*

*Is this the **right** house?*   *Halloween is next **week**.*

Underline the correct homophone in each sentence.

1. Make a (write right) turn on Clark Street.

2. Alexa is a (deer dear) friend.

3. The (see sea) is very rough today.

4. There was a (deer dear) in our yard.

5. The branch fell because it was (week weak).

6. I should (write right) to my grandma.

7. May I (see sea) the dinosaur bone?

8. I have piano lessons every (week weak).

Writer's Corner

Write two sentences about yourself. Use the homophones *write* and *right*.

Practice Working with Homophones

Complete each sentence. Use a homophone of a word on the right.

1. The story tells how the elephant got its _____ .   **dear**

2. Isabel could _____ the robins singing.   **tale**

3. Caleb _____ at a Mexican restaurant.   **our**

4. We spent an _____ in the dinosaur museum.   **here**

5. A strange animal passed _____ .   **buy**

6. I saw a _____ in the woods.   **sea**

7. I can _____ Venus through this telescope.   **knew**

8. Katelyn got a _____ bike for Christmas.   **eight**

Homophones, homophones,
we know quite a few.
Dear and *deer*, *here* and *hear*,
to and *two* and *too*.
Homophones, homophones,
how *our* list will grow.
Words that we call homophones
are jolly friends to know.

Homophones Review

A Read each sentence. If the underlined homophone is correct, put an **X** on the line. If the homophone is not correct, write the correct homophone on the line.

1. I <u>knew</u> we were going to the zoo! _____

2. Did you <u>here</u> about the field trip? _____

3. I'm going to <u>right</u> in my notebook. _____

4. Where did you <u>buy</u> that sweater? _____

5. There are <u>ate</u> apples in the basket. _____

B Underline the correct homophone in each sentence.

1. This is (our hour) favorite story.

2. I love swimming in the (see sea).

3. A letter begins with (Dear Deer).

4. I'll see you next (weak week).

5. Will you (bee be) long?

6. Where should we (meet meat)?

7. That monkey has a long (tale tail).

Name _____

Show What You Know

A **Find a synonym in the list for each underlined word. Write the letter on the line.**

1. Riley is <u>afraid</u> of the dark. _____   a. pull

2. Did Dad <u>discover</u> the beavers' home? _____   b. find

3. Be <u>quiet</u>. _____   c. hurt

4. Can lightning <u>harm</u> you? _____   d. silent

5. Jamie started to <u>tug</u> at his mother's skirt. _____   e. scared

B **For each set, draw a line from each word in the first list to its antonym in the second list.**

1. dry ●   ● weak
2. full ●   ● last
3. strong ●   ● empty
4. small ●   ● wet
5. first ●   ● large

1. tall ●   ● low
2. high ●   ● light
3. inside ●   ● never
4. heavy ●   ● outside
5. always ●   ● short

Name _____

Show What You Know

Ⓐ Underline the antonyms in each sentence.

1. Does Chad live near the lake or far from the lake?

2. Did the dog go over or under the fence?

3. Is the pizza crust thick or thin?

4. Was your answer right or wrong?

5. Shall I open or close the window?

6. Is your sister happy today, or is she sad?

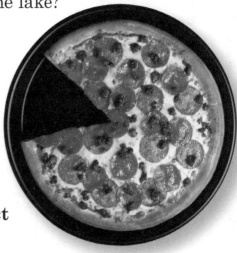

Ⓑ Complete each sentence with the correct homophone.

eight
ate

sea
see

hear
here

Write
Right

tale
tail

new
knew

1. Look at the dolphin swimming in the _____ .

2. Our school has a _____ computer.

3. Can you _____ the hoot of the owl?

4. Henry wore the number _____ on his shirt.

5. A monkey can swing by its _____ .

6. _____ your name at the top of your paper.

Get Ready to Write

What Is a Research Report?

A **research report** tells facts about one topic. A research report can tell about a person, a place, a thing, or an event.

The **beginning** of a research report names the topic.

The **middle** of a research report tells more about the topic. Information about the topic comes from different sources.

The **ending** of a research report sums up the report.

Beginning — A brachiosaurus is a kind of dinosaur. It was 40 feet tall and 80 feet long. It weighed 60 tons. The brachiosaurus ate plants. Bones of the brachiosaurus have been found in Colorado. A brachiosaurus skeleton is on display in Chicago.

Middle

Ending — The brachiosaurus was a huge, gentle dinosaur.

○ **Answer these questions about the research report.**

1. What is the topic of the research report?

_____

_____

2. What fact told what the brachiosaurus ate?

_____

_____

3. What does the ending say about the topic?

_____

_____

_____

The Topic of a Research Report

A research report is about one **topic**. The topic is something you want to know more about. It can be about a person, a place, a thing, or an event.

The **beginning** of a research report has a **topic sentence**. A topic sentence tells what your research report is about. A topic sentence should grab the reader's attention. It should make the reader want to learn more.

Look at these topic sentences. Each one tells about a topic. But some sentences are more interesting than others.

I have a goldfish.

Goldfish are one of the most popular pets.

My report is about walking sticks.

A walking stick is an insect that looks like a stick.

The Statue of Liberty is cool.

The Statue of Liberty is a huge statue in New York.

Look at each topic. Write your own topic sentence. Try to grab the reader's attention.

1. **zebras**

_____

_____

2. **firefighters**

_____

_____

Fact and Opinion

The **middle** of your research report gives **facts**. A fact is something that is true. You can get facts from books, encyclopedias, or on the Internet.

Be sure your report doesn't give your **opinion**. An opinion tells what you think or feel.

FACT: *Polar bears have black skin under their fur.*

OPINION: *I like polar bears.*

A Read each sentence. Underline **F** if the sentence is a fact. Underline **O** if the sentence is an opinion.

Polar bears are not really white.   **F**   **O**

I'd like to see a polar bear.   **F**   **O**

Polar bears eat meat.   **F**   **O**

I think it would be fun to have a polar bear.   **F**   **O**

Polar bears are my favorite animal.   **F**   **O**

Black skin helps the polar bear stay warm.   **F**   **O**

B Circle one of these topics. Write three facts about it. Find facts in books, in encyclopedias, or on the Internet.

dinosaurs   Thanksgiving   pirates

FACT: _____

FACT: _____

FACT: _____

Finding Facts

You can find facts in the library. You look for facts in **sources**. Some sources you can look in are encyclopedias, nonfiction books, and the Internet. Write the facts in your own words.

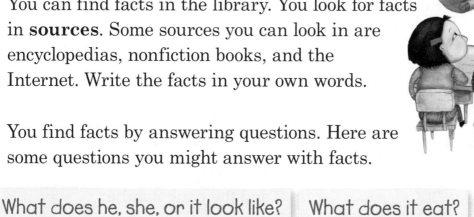

You find facts by answering questions. Here are some questions you might answer with facts.

What does he, she, or it look like?   What does it eat?   Where is it?

Where does he, she, or it live?   How big is it?   What did he or she do?

Choose one of these topics. Find three facts about the topic. Find one fact in each kind of source.

spiders   tigers   George Washington   Alaska

Fact 1: _____

nonfiction book _____

_____

Fact 2: _____

encyclopedia _____

_____

Fact 3: _____

the Internet _____

_____

Writing and Organizing Notes

As you find facts, write them down. Write them in your own words on note cards.

Write the fact at the top of the note card. Write where you found the fact at the bottom of the note card.

If the fact is from	Write
a book	the title, the author, and the page number
an encyclopedia	the article title, the encyclopedia name, the volume number, and the page number
the Internet	the web address

After you have taken notes, put the cards into piles. Make a pile for each kind of information that you have. Note cards might look like this.

Red pandas live in Nepal, Burma, and central China.
"Red Pandas." Encyclopedia Britannica. Vol. 2, p. 245

Red pandas weigh less than 20 pounds.
www.tigerhomes.org/animal/redpanda.cfm

Look at the facts that you wrote on page 201. Write each fact at the top of a separate note card. Write where you found the fact at the bottom. Then find three more facts. Write a note card for each fact. Put your cards into piles. Put facts that go together in the same pile.

Writing an Ending

In the **ending** you sum up your research report.

Look at these endings. Which endings do you think are better?

Some goldfish are orange.

Goldfish are good pets because they are easy to take care of.

I'm glad I chose this topic.

Walking sticks are bugs with clever costumes.

So now you know what I know about the Statue of Liberty.

The Statue of Liberty is one of the most visited places in New York.

Read the research reports below. Add an ending sentence to each.

Abraham Lincoln worked his whole life to end slavery. Many people did not agree with him. Southern states wanted to keep slavery. Lincoln's army fought the Southern armies. Finally Lincoln made the Emancipation Proclamation. It freed the slaves.

The crew of Apollo 11 made the first mission to the moon. Neil Armstrong, Michael Collins, and Edwin "Buzz" Aldrin were the crew. The trip from Earth to the moon took four days. Neil Armstrong took the first step on the moon.

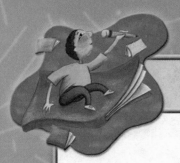

Writer's Workshop

PREWRITING

Pick a Topic

Cady is writing a research report. A research report has facts. First Cady must pick a topic. Cady thinks about things she would like to know more about. She lists them in her notebook.

skateboarding

the Pilgrims

blue whales

Florence Nightingale

Cady circles the topic she likes best. This is the topic she will write about.

Make a list of topics. Think about people, places, things, and events. Is the topic something you want to know more about? Is it something you can find a lot of information about? Is it something others might want to know more about? Circle the topic you want to write about.

PREWRITING

Plan Your Research Report

Cady plans her research report. First she goes to the library. She finds facts in an encyclopedia. She finds more facts on the Internet. The librarian helps her find Web sites that have good information.

Then Cady writes each fact on a separate note card. She puts the note cards into piles. One pile is about what blue whales eat. The other pile is about the size of blue whales.

Do research in the library. Find facts about your topic. Write each fact on a separate note card. Write the facts in your own words. Remember to write where you found each fact.

When you have finished, put the note cards into piles. Did you write about an animal, like Cady did? Make one pile with facts about what the animal looks like. Make another pile about what the animal eats. Make a third pile about where the animal lives.

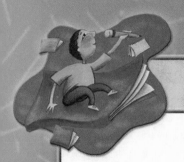

Writer's Workshop

DRAFTING

Cady wrote a lot of note cards. She uses her cards to write her report. Here is Cady's draft.

An Enormous Animal

The blue whale is the largest animal on Earth. It lives in the see. Some blue whales weigh 200 tons. A blue whale's tongue can weigh as much as an elephant. A blue whale's food is called krill. Krill are very tiny animals that are like shrimp. Blue whales can eat 12,000 pounds of krill a day. I think blue whales are really cool.

Write your draft in your notebook. Remember to write a topic sentence that grabs the reader's attention. Write in the middle of your report the facts that you found. Include facts that your reader might want to know. Write an ending that sums up the topic. Remember that you can make changes to your draft later.

EDITING

Cady must edit her research report. She wants to make sure it makes sense and has all its parts.

Cady uses this Editing Checklist. She checks one question at a time.

like shrimp. Blue whales can eat 12,000 pounds of krill a day. ~~I think blue whales are really cool.~~ The blue whale is the largest animal, but it eats some of the smallest food.

Look at the mistake Cady finds. How does she fix it?

Use the Editing Checklist to edit your report. Check for one question at a time. When you have finished, read aloud your research report. Can you add anything to make your report better? Mark your changes on your draft.

I didn't leave out my opinion!

REVISING

Cady fixes the mistakes she marked. Then she makes a new copy of her draft.

Copy your draft. Fix any mistakes you marked. Make sure you can answer yes to all the questions on the checklist.

Writer's Workshop

PROOFREADING

Cady wants to proofread her research report. By proofreading she will catch even more mistakes. She uses this Proofreading Checklist. She carefully checks one question at a time.

Proofreading Checklist

☐ Are all the words spelled correctly?

☐ Did I use capital letters?

☐ Did I use the right end marks?

☐ Can I replace any words with synonyms?

☐ Are antonyms used correctly?

☐ Are all homophones used correctly?

An Enormous Animal

The blue whale is the largest animal on Earth.
                          sea
It lives in the ⌃see. Some blue whales weigh 200

tons. A blue whale's tongue can weigh as much as

Look at the mistake Cady finds. How does she fix it?

Use the Proofreading Checklist to check your draft. Look for one kind of mistake at a time. Make your words and sentences as clear as you can. Remember to read over your draft to make sure that you did not add any new mistakes.

PUBLISHING

After all her hard work, Cady is excited to publish her report.
She writes the final copy. Then she draws a picture of a blue whale
on the cover of her report. Cady publishes her report by reading it
to her class.

Recopy your research report. Write as neatly as you can.
Make sure that you did not add any new mistakes.
Remember to add a title.

Now decide how to publish our research report.
Here are some ways you might publish it.
Can you think of other ways?

Read your report
to your class.

Make a class magazine.

Make a classroom encyclopedia.
Include everyone's research reports.

Hang your report on a
classroom bulletin board.

Research Tools

Computer Area

Fiction Section

A-L

Librarian

Circulation Desk

BEARS

Book Return

Nonfiction Section

Reference Area

Reading Area

Name _____

Alphabetical Order

Words in **alphabetical order** are in the order of the letters of the alphabet. These words are in order by the first letter of each word.

*a*stronaut   *m*oon   *p*lanets   *s*pace

● These children have to line up in alphabetical order. Write their names in alphabetical order. Use their last names.

1. _____

2. _____

3. _____

4. _____

5. _____

6. _____

7. _____

8. _____

Brandon Deane

Sarah Fowler

Nancy Wright

Miguel Covas

Audrey Anders

Luis Gonzalez

Jenna Roth

Seth Baker

Name _____

More Alphabetical Order

Words that start with the same letter are put in alphabetical order by the second letter.

    *b*a*ll*   *b*e*ep*   *b*i*g*   *b*o*x*

A Are these names in alphabetical order? Write yes or no.

  1. Aiden, Abigail, Andrew   _____

  2. Ella, Emma, Ethan   _____

  3. Caleb, Chloe, Connor   _____

  4. Molly, Mitch, Matt   _____

  5. Gerry, Gia, Grace   _____

B Look at the words in the word bank. Write them in alphabetical order.

bear	bison	bat
bobcat	bumblebee	bluebird

1. _____   4. _____

2. _____   5. _____

3. _____   6. _____

Practice with Alphabetical Order

A Put each group of words in alphabetical order. Write 1, 2, 3, or 4 next to each word to show the correct order.

1. squid _____

   sea _____

   orca _____

   turtle _____

2. bat _____

   tiger _____

   fox _____

   bear _____

B Write each group of words in alphabetical order.

1. almost _____

   add _____

   any _____

   apple _____

2. grass _____

   goat _____

   gave _____

   get _____

3. more _____

   music _____

   miss _____

   meet _____

4. she _____

   snow _____

   story _____

   seal _____

Dictionary Skills

A **dictionary** is a book of words. A dictionary tells you how to spell a word and what a word means. The words in a dictionary are in alphabetical order.

guide words

garden — — — — — — — — — — — — — — — **gym**

entry —

garden   a piece of ground used for growing
vegetables, flowers, or fruits
*We have a big **garden** in our yard.*

germ   something that can make
a person sick
*A **germ** has given me a cold.*

give   to let someone have something
*Did she **give** you the balloons?*

gym   a big room used for exercise
or playing games
*We play basketball in the **gym**.*

meaning

1. What letter does each word start with? _____

2. Which word comes before **give** in the dictionary? _____

3. Which word comes after **give** in the dictionary? _____

Dictionary Skills—Parts of an Entry

A dictionary **entry** has at least two parts: the **entry word** and the **meaning**. A dictionary may use a picture or an example sentence to help you understand what the word means. This is a dictionary entry.

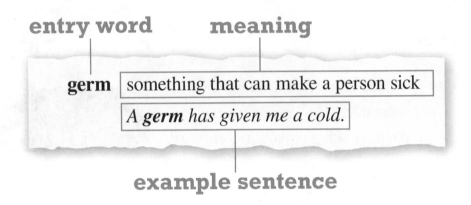

entry word   **meaning**

germ   something that can make a person sick

A **germ** has given me a cold.

example sentence

Use the **dictionary page on page 215** to answer these questions.

1. Which entry word means **a big room used for exercise or playing games**?

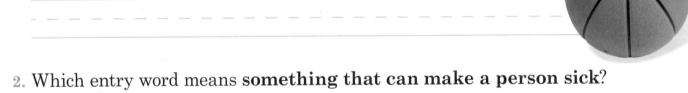

2. Which entry word means **something that can make a person sick?**

3. Write the meaning of the word **give.**

4. Write your own example sentence for the word **garden.**

Dictionary Skills—Guide Words

Guide words help you find a word in a dictionary. Guide words are at the top corners of each page. They tell the first and last words on a dictionary page.

> **When you look for a word in a dictionary, do the following:**
>
> 1. Decide if the word is in the beginning, the middle, or the end of the dictionary.
> 2. Look at the guide words.
> 3. Decide if your word comes alphabetically between the two guide words.
> 4. If it does, look for the word on the page.

A **Where would you find each word? Write beginning, middle, or end.**

1. ball _____
2. maid _____
3. dog _____
4. yawn _____
5. zoo _____
6. limp _____

B **Read each pair of guide words. Underline the word that you might find on a page with those guide words.**

1. caterpillar—check   cent   hold   build
2. dragon—dust   salad   dress   nurse
3. fall—finger   horse   fast   barn
4. hair—heart   head   bird   carrot
5. idea—invent   tree   gate   insect
6. pig—pizza   pill   flower   pull

Name _____

Encyclopedia Skills

An **encyclopedia** is a group of books that has information. The information is about people, places, things, and events. Each book is called a **volume**. The topics in an encyclopedia are in alphabetical order. Each topic is called an **entry**.

entry

Encyclopedia of Knowledge

F
volume
6

volume

Frog, Northern Cricket
Cricket frogs are tree frogs. They do not climb, and they have no pads on their toes. Northern cricket frogs can vary in color from frog to frog. They are small, with warty skin and a dark triangle between their eyes. Often they have dark spots or stripes. They make a sound like two small stones being quickly tapped together.

The northern cricket frog breeds in spring and early summer. Even though these frogs come out during the day, their small size can make them difficult to find.

● **Answer these questions about the encyclopedia entry above.**

1. What is the topic of this entry?

_____

_____

2. In which volume can this entry be found? _____

_____

3. What type of frog is the northern cricket frog? _____

4. Write one interesting fact you learned about the northern cricket frog.

_____

Fiction and Nonfiction Books

Fiction books tell about make-believe people, places, things, or events. These books are on library shelves in alphabetical order by the author's last name. Fiction books are in a special part of the library.

Nonfiction books tell about real people, places, things, and events. These books tell facts. They are on library shelves by topic. They are in a different part of the library.

Can you tell which books are nonfiction and which books are fiction? Write nonfiction or fiction after each title.

1. Perry and the Pink Lion

2. Lions in Africa

3. Where Lions Live

4. A Lion's Wearing My Shoes!

5. How Lions Live

6. The Lion's Tea Party

7. The Tale of the Lion and the Ant

8. The Truth About Lions

Name _____

Parts of a Book

A book has many parts. The **cover** tells the title and the author of the book. The **contents page** tells where to find information about a topic.

title

page

topic

Contents

Chapter

1. Earthworms 1

2. Worms That Recycle 15

3. Leeches 27

4. Tapeworms 40

All About Worms

by James Carlson

author

○ **Answer these questions about the parts of a book.**

1. What is the title of the book?

_____

_____

2. Who is the author of the book?

_____

_____

3. Which chapter has facts about worms that recycle?

_____

_____

4. On what page would you start looking for facts about leeches?

_____

_____

Name

Using the Internet

Some people call the **Internet** the world's biggest library. You can use the Internet to find facts about any topic that you research.

Make sure that the information you find on the Internet is true. Sometimes what you read on the Internet is made up. Use **search engines** made for kids. A kids' search engine helps you find Web sites that have true information.

Internet safety is very important. Don't give out information about yourself, such as your name or your address. Make sure a grown-up is nearby when you are using the Internet. If you see something that makes you uncomfortable, tell a grown-up.

Grammar Review

A Read these sentences. Tell what kind of sentence each sentence is.

t = telling   c = commanding   a = asking   e = exclaiming

1. The thunder scared me! _____
2. I caught a fish. _____
3. Go to bed. _____
4. Do you have a pet? _____
5. We drink lemonade. _____
6. Call your grandma. _____
7. What time is it? _____
8. I love this song! _____

B Underline the correct month in each sentence.

1. It is cold in (October Oktobur).
2. We swim in (Jewly July).
3. (March June) is before April.
4. Flowers grow in (May Mae).
5. School is out in (January June).
6. (December May) is the last month.

C Circle the abbreviation or the initials in each sentence. Then add periods.

1. T M S are his initials.
2. J J B are her initials.
3. Mr Martinez has a garden.
4. Mar means March.
5. Thur means Thursday.
6. Dr Roy will see you now.

D Read these sentences. Write **p** if the underlined word is a pronoun. Write **a** if the underlined word is an adjective.

1. His name is Mark. _____
2. Kat ate the crunchy apple. _____
3. Where did she go? _____
4. Are you going home? _____
5. What bright snow! _____
6. Jay has nine plums. _____

Name _____

E **Read each sentence. Underline the common noun. Circle the proper noun.**

1. Molly reads a lot of books.

2. The snake looked at Ellie.

3. The nearby lake is Lake Michigan.

4. Julian found a quarter.

5. The dog jumped on Sophia.

6. Ellie bought a camera.

F **Underline the correct contraction for the two words.**

1. could not   can't   couldn't

2. I have   I've   I'll

3. has not   hasn't   hadn't

4. I am   I'll   I'm

5. we had   we're   we'd

6. they are   they'd   they're

7. we have   we've   we'd

8. you are   you'd   you're

G **Underline the correct verb in each sentence.**

1. Eve (open opens) the jar.

2. I (have has) a map.

3. A pumpkin (have has) seeds.

4. I (climbs climbed) the tree yesterday.

5. Grandpa (will was) build a fire.

6. The team is (play playing) well.

7. Who has (saw seen) my mitten?

8. They have (ate eaten) breakfast.

9. Tomas has (gave given) me a gift.

10. He was (went gone) that day.

11. Our chores were (did done) early.

12. The pizza (is am) cold.

13. I (is am) a fast runner.

14. A fish (was were) in the pond.

Acknowledgments

Illustration

Anni Betts: 9, 14, 28, 30, 31, 46, 58, 59, 61, 89, 92, 102, 116, 127 top, 131, 156, 176–177, 204, 219, 221

Holli Conger: iii bottom, 18, 25, 32, 33, 42 top, 51, 57 top, 78, 79, 87, 112, 118, 132, 144–145, 170, 184, 189

Deborah Melman: iv top, v bottom, 10, 13, 40–41, 56, 77, 88, 95, 114, 122 top, 155, 158, 181, 195, 210–211

Cindy Revell: iii middle, 8, 11, 16, 19, 20, 21, 24, 27, 29, 42 bottom, 43, 45, 47, 49, 52, 57 bottom, 60, 62, 63, 76, 81, 84, 85, 86, 91, 94, 96, 99, 110–111, 117, 121, 122 bottom, 126, 127 middle, 128, 133, 146, 151, 159, 162, 163, 164, 178, 183, 188, 190, 192, 194, 196, 201, 212

Christine Schneider: 6–7, 48, 53, 64, 80, 93, 98, 113, 123, 129, 138–139, 149, 167, 179, 193, 203, 214

Melanie Siegel: iv middle, 17, 23, 44, 50, 54, 74–75, 97, 115, 124, 136, 154, 187, 198, 215

Photography

Phil Martin Photography: 37, 39, 41, 71, 73, 107, 109, 141, 143, 173, 175, 207, 209

© **Lynda Richardson/CORBIS:** 218

Literature

Quote from Joseph Addison found in *Scholastic Treasury of Quotations for Children*. Copyright © by Adrienne Betz. Published by Scholastic Inc. All rights reserved.

Loyola Press has made every effort to locate the copyright holders for the cited works used in this publication and to make full acknowledgment for their use. In the case of any omissions, the Publisher will be pleased to make suitable acknowledgments in future editions.